FAST
chicken

THE AUSTRALIAN
Women's Weekly

FAST
chicken

acp
books

contents

Chicken is such a great-tasting and versatile meat that it could easily be the main ingredient of a meal several times a week for ages without you getting bored or having to duplicate a recipe. The numerous cuts, plus mince, are easy and quick to prepare, and chicken, when compared with other meats, is relatively inexpensive, and low in fat and cholesterol. Some of the cuts in this book are: **breast fillet** skinless and boneless; **tenderloin** thin strip of meat under breast; **thigh cutlet** skin-on, one bone; **thigh fillet** skinless and boneless; **wing** skin-on, bones intact; **drumstick** leg skin-on, bones intact; **drumette** wing trimmed to resemble small drumstick; **maryland** connected leg/thigh piece with bones and skin; **strips** boneless, skinless stir-fry-size pieces of thigh or breast meat; and **mince** ground thigh or breast meat. We've also included a chapter using purchased barbecued chicken. It's very important that chicken is kept under refrigeration until you're ready to cook it; always defrost frozen chicken in the refrigerator, and never keep raw chicken in the refrigerator for more than 2 days at the most.

grills+
barbecues

Chicken with capers, anchovies and rosemary

¼ cup (50g) capers, rinsed, drained, chopped finely
4 cloves garlic, crushed
6 anchovies, chopped finely
2 teaspoons fresh rosemary leaves
8 thigh cutlets (1.3kg)

1 Combine capers, garlic, anchovies and rosemary in small bowl.
2 Preheat grill to hot.
3 Cut two deep slashes through skin and flesh of chicken. Place a teaspoon of caper mixture into each of the slashes.
4 Cook chicken under hot grill until chicken is browned both sides and cooked through.
5 Serve chicken with salad leaves and steamed baby potatoes, if desired.

on the table in 35 minutes
serves 4 **per serving** 32.8g total fat (10.8g saturated fat); 1906kJ (456 cal); 1.3g carbohydrate; 39.0g protein; 0.7g fibre

Chicken with nam jim

8 thigh cutlets (1.3kg)
⅓ cup (90g) grated palm sugar
2 teaspoons ground cumin
1 cup loosely packed fresh mint leaves
1 cup loosely packed fresh thai basil leaves
nam jim
2 cloves garlic, quartered
3 long green chillies, chopped coarsely
2 coriander roots
2 tablespoons fish sauce
2 tablespoons grated palm sugar
3 shallots (75g), chopped coarsely
¼ cup (60ml) lime juice

1 Cut two deep slashes through skin and flesh of chicken; rub chicken with combined sugar and cumin.
2 Cook chicken, on heated oiled grill plate (or grill or barbecue) until browned all over and cooked through.
3 Meanwhile, make nam jim.
4 Serve chicken with herbs and nam jim.
nam jim blend or process ingredients until smooth.

on the table in 35 minutes
serves 4 **per serving** 16.7g total fat (5.0g saturated fat); 1889kJ (452 cal); 30.2g carbohydrate; 44.3g protein; 1.8g fibre

Sweet and sour chicken

4 breast fillets (800g)
440g can pineapple pieces in natural juice
1 tablespoon peanut oil
1 small brown onion (80g), sliced thinly
1 large red capsicum (350g), chopped coarsely
1 large green capsicum (350g), chopped coarsely
1 trimmed celery stalk (100g), sliced thickly
¼ cup (60ml) tomato sauce
¼ cup (60ml) plum sauce
2 tablespoons light soy sauce
¼ cup (60ml) white vinegar
1 tablespoon cornflour
½ cup (125ml) chicken stock

1 Cook chicken on heated oiled grill plate (or grill or barbecue) until browned all over and cooked through; slice thickly. Cover to keep warm.
2 Drain pineapple; reserve juice.
3 Heat oil in large saucepan; cook pineapple, onion, capsicums and celery, stirring, 4 minutes. Add reserved juice, sauces, vinegar and blended cornflour and stock; stir until mixture boils and thickens slightly.
4 Serve chicken topped with sweet and sour sauce.

on the table in 20 minutes
serves 4 **per serving** 9.7g total fat (2.1g saturated fat); 1764kJ (422 cal); 31.4g carbohydrate; 49.5g protein; 4.1g fibre

Chicken tenderloins in green peppercorn and tarragon dressing

4 medium potatoes (800g)
600g tenderloins
1 tablespoon cracked black pepper
4 large tomatoes (1kg), sliced thinly
1 medium red onion (170g), sliced thinly
green peppercorn and tarragon dressing
2 tablespoons water
2 teaspoons drained green peppercorns, crushed
2 teaspoons wholegrain mustard
2 green onions, sliced thinly
1 tablespoon coarsely chopped fresh tarragon
1 tablespoon olive oil
1 tablespoon white sugar
⅓ cup (80ml) white wine vinegar

1 Make green peppercorn and tarragon dressing.
2 Boil, steam or microwave potatoes until just tender; drain.
3 Meanwhile, coat chicken all over in black pepper. Cook chicken on heated oiled grill plate (or grill or barbecue) until browned all over and cooked through; slice thickly.
4 When potatoes are cool enough to handle, slice thickly. Cook potato, in batches, on same heated oiled grill plate until browned both sides.
5 Arrange chicken, potato, tomato and onion slices on serving plates; drizzle with dressing.
green peppercorn and tarragon dressing place ingredients in screw-top jar; shake well.

on the table in 25 minutes
serves 4 **per serving** 13.4g total fat (3.2g saturated fat); 1797kJ (430 cal); 34.1g carbohydrate; 39.6g protein; 6.6g fibre

17

Mustard and rosemary chicken

4 breast fillets (800g)
1 tablespoon wholegrain mustard
1 tablespoon lemon juice
1 tablespoon olive oil
1 tablespoon finely chopped fresh rosemary
1 clove garlic, crushed
600g tiny new potatoes, quartered
250g baby spinach leaves
20g butter
1 medium lemon (140g), quartered

1 Combine chicken, mustard, juice, oil, rosemary and garlic in medium bowl.
2 Cook chicken mixture on heated oiled grill plate (or grill or barbecue) until browned all over and cooked through.
3 Meanwhile, boil, steam or microwave potato until just tender; drain. Place hot potato in large bowl with spinach and butter; toss gently until butter melts and spinach just wilts.
4 Serve chicken with vegetables and lemon quarters.

on the table in 20 minutes
serves 4 **per serving** 13.8g total fat (4.5g saturated fat); 1764kJ (422 cal); 20.7g carbohydrate; 50.8g protein; 5.2g fibre
tip you will need two lemons for this recipe.

Chicken tikka wrap

2 breast fillets (400g)
1 tablespoon tikka paste
2½ cups (700g) yogurt
2 lebanese cucumbers (260g), seeded, chopped finely
⅓ cup coarsely chopped fresh mint
1 small red onion (100g), chopped finely
4 large pitta bread
100g mesclun

1 Cut each fillet in half horizontally. Combine chicken in large bowl with paste and 2 tablespoons of the yogurt.
2 Cook chicken mixture on heated oiled grill plate (or grill or barbecue) until browned all over and cooked through; slice thinly.
3 Combine cucumber, mint, onion and remaining yogurt in medium bowl.
4 Spread yogurt mixture over whole of each piece of bread; top with equal amounts of mesclun then chicken. Roll to enclose filling.

on the table in 35 minutes
serves 4 **per serving** 11.9g total fat (4.8g saturated fat); 2011kJ (481 cal); 51.1g carbohydrate; 39.2g protein; 4.5g fibre

Stuffed chicken breast with spinach salad

4 breast fillets (800g)
80g fontina cheese, sliced thinly
4 slices bottled char-grilled red capsicum (170g)
100g baby spinach leaves
1 medium lemon (140g)
2 medium oranges (480g)
1 small red onion (100g), sliced thinly
1 tablespoon olive oil

1 Using tip of small knife, slit a pocket in one side of each fillet, taking care not to cut all the way through. Divide cheese, capsicum and a few spinach leaves among pockets; secure with toothpicks.
2 Cook chicken on heated oiled grill plate (or grill or barbecue) until browned all over and cooked through. Cover chicken; stand 10 minutes. Remove toothpicks; slice thickly.
3 Meanwhile, segment lemon and orange over large bowl, add onion, oil and remaining spinach; toss gently to combine.
4 Serve chicken with salad.

on the table in 30 minutes
serves 4 **per serving** 14.8g total fat (5.3g saturated fat); 1664kJ (398 cal); 10.7g carbohydrate; 53.3g protein; 3.8g fibre

Coriander and chilli grilled fillets

6 thigh fillets (660g), halved
coriander chilli sauce
8 green onions, chopped coarsely
3 cloves garlic, quartered
3 fresh small red thai chillies, chopped coarsely
¼ cup loosely packed fresh coriander leaves
1 teaspoon white sugar
1 tablespoon fish sauce
¼ cup (60ml) lime juice
chickpea salad
2 x 300g cans chickpeas, rinsed, drained
2 medium egg tomatoes (150g), chopped coarsely
2 green onions, chopped finely
2 tablespoons lime juice
1 cup coarsely chopped fresh coriander
1 tablespoon olive oil

1 Make coriander chilli sauce.
2 Cook chicken on heated oiled grill plate (or grill or barbecue) until almost cooked through. Brush about two-thirds of the coriander chilli sauce all over chicken; cook further 5 minutes or until chicken is cooked through.
3 Make chickpea salad.
4 Serve chicken, sprinkled with remaining coriander chilli sauce and chickpea salad.
coriander chilli sauce blend or process onion, garlic, chilli, coriander and sugar until finely chopped. Add fish sauce and juice; blend until well combined.
chickpea salad place ingredients in large bowl; toss to combine.

on the table in 25 minutes
serves 4 **per serving** 18.5g total fat (4.6g saturated fat); 1651kJ (395 cal); 15.9g carbohydrate; 38.3g protein; 6.2g fibre

Grilled chicken wings with ranch dressing and rocket and blue cheese salad

12 wings (1kg)
1 tablespoon olive oil
ranch dressing
⅓ cup (95g) yogurt
⅓ cup (100g) mayonnaise
2 tablespoons buttermilk
1 small brown onion (80g), grated finely
1 clove garlic, crushed
1 tablespoon finely chopped fresh chives
rocket and blue cheese salad
100g baby rocket leaves
250g grape tomatoes, halved
1 tablespoon olive oil
2 tablespoons red wine vinegar
100g blue cheese, cut into 4 wedges

1 Cut wing tips from chicken; discard tips. Cut wings in half at joints. Brush chicken with oil; cook on heated oiled grill plate (or grill or barbecue) until browned all over and cooked through.
2 Meanwhile, make ranch dressing.
3 Make rocket and blue cheese salad.
4 Serve chicken with salad and ranch dressing.
ranch dressing combine ingredients in small bowl.
rocket and blue cheese salad combine rocket, tomato, oil and vinegar in medium bowl; top with cheese.

on the table in 30 minutes
serves 4 **per serving** 34.9g total fat (10.8g saturated fat); 2220kJ (531 cal); 9.8g carbohydrate; 44.2g protein; 1.9g fibre
tip buy the best quality whole-egg mayonnaise you can find for this recipe (if you don't make your own) because the sweetness of some commercial mayonnaise will spoil the taste of the ranch dressing.

Chicken tandoori pockets with raita

400g tenderloins
1 tablespoon lime juice
⅓ cup (100g) tandoori paste
¼ cup (70g) yogurt
8 large flour tortillas
60g snow pea sprouts
raita
1 cup (280g) yogurt
1 lebanese cucumber (130g), halved, seeded, chopped finely
1 tablespoon finely chopped fresh mint

1 Make raita.
2 Combine chicken, juice, paste and yogurt in medium bowl.
3 Cook chicken mixture on heated oiled grill plate (or grill or barbecue) until browned all over and cooked through; slice thickly.
4 Heat tortillas according to manufacturer's instructions.
5 Place equal amounts of chicken, sprouts and raita on a quarter section of each tortilla; fold tortilla in half and then in half again to enclose filling and form triangle-shaped pockets.
raita combine ingredients in small bowl.

on the table in 25 minutes
makes 8 **per pocket** 22.9g total fat (5.4g saturated fat); 2445kJ (585 cal); 55.8g carbohydrate; 35.5g protein; 6.2g fibre

Chicken with herbed butter, almonds and gruyère

80g butter, softened
1 tablespoon finely chopped fresh flat-leaf parsley
2 teaspoons lemon juice
4 breast fillets (800g)
3 medium carrots (360g), cut into 8cm-long matchsticks
250g baby green beans
¼ cup (35g) toasted slivered almonds
¼ cup (30g) finely grated gruyère cheese

1 Combine butter, parsley and juice in small bowl. Cover; refrigerate.
2 Cook chicken on heated oiled grill plate (or grill or barbecue) until browned all over and cooked through. Cover loosely to keep warm.
3 Meanwhile, boil, steam or microwave carrot and beans, separately, until tender; drain.
4 Serve chicken on vegetables; divide parsley butter among chicken pieces, sprinkle with nuts and cheese.

on the table in 35 minutes
serves 4 **per serving** 28.1g total fat (13.6g saturated fat); 2052kJ (491 cal); 6.2g carbohydrate; 51.2g protein; 4.8g fibre

Chutney chicken breast with kashmiri pilaf

1 tablespoon vegetable oil
1 small brown onion (80g), chopped finely
1 clove garlic, crushed
1 teaspoon black mustard seeds
¼ teaspoon ground cardamom
½ teaspoon ground cumin
½ teaspoon garam masala
½ teaspoon ground turmeric
1½ cups (300g) long-grain white rice
3 cups (750ml) chicken stock
2 tablespoons coarsely chopped fresh coriander
⅓ cup (80g) mango chutney
2 tablespoons water
4 breast fillets (800g)

1 Heat oil in medium saucepan; cook onion, garlic and mustard seeds, stirring, until onion softens and seeds pop. Add remaining spices; cook, stirring, until fragrant.
2 Add rice; stir to coat in spices. Add stock; bring to a boil. Reduce heat, simmer, uncovered, until rice is just tender. Stir in coriander; keep warm.
3 Meanwhile, cook chutney and the water in small saucepan, stirring, until heated through.
4 Cook chicken, brushing all over with chutney mixture, on heated oiled grill plate (or grill or barbecue) until browned all over and cooked through. Cut into thick slices.
5 Serve chutney chicken with pilaf.

on the table in 30 minutes
serves 4 **per serving** 17.1g total fat (4.2g saturated fat); 2625kJ (628 cal); 70.6g carbohydrate; 46.3g protein; 1.5g fibre
tip mango chutney will burn if the grill or barbecue is too hot.

Asian chicken burger with wasabi mayonnaise

1 lebanese cucumber (130g), sliced thinly
¼ cup (70g) drained pickled pink ginger
½ cup (125ml) rice vinegar
1 teaspoon salt
1 tablespoon white sugar
500g mince
2cm piece fresh ginger (10g), grated
1 tablespoon soy sauce
1 egg
1 cup (70g) stale breadcrumbs
1 teaspoon sesame oil
2 green onions, chopped finely
4 hamburger buns
50g mizuna
wasabi mayonnaise
¼ cup (75g) mayonnaise
2 teaspoons wasabi paste

1 Combine cucumber in small bowl with pickled ginger, vinegar, salt and sugar; set aside until required.
2 Using hand, combine mince, fresh ginger, sauce, egg, breadcrumbs, oil and onion in large bowl; shape mixture into four patties.
3 Cook patties on heated oiled flat plate (or barbecue) until browned all over and cooked through.
4 Meanwhile, split buns in half horizontally; toast, cut-side up.
5 Make wasabi mayonnaise; spread on bun bases.
6 Sandwich mizuna, patties and drained cucumber mixture between bun halves.
wasabi mayonnaise combine ingredients in small bowl.

on the table in 35 minutes
serves 4 **per serving** 22g total fat (4.8g saturated fat); 2399kJ (574 cal); 57.7g carbohydrate; 35.2g protein; 1.3g fibre

Chicken, lemon and artichoke skewers

2 tablespoons lemon juice
2 tablespoons olive oil
2 cloves garlic, crushed
2 medium lemons (280g)
500g breast fillets, cut into 3cm pieces
2 x 400g cans artichoke hearts, drained, halved
24 button mushrooms (300g)

1 Place juice, oil and garlic in screw-top jar; shake well.
2 Cut lemons into 24 pieces. Thread chicken, artichoke, mushrooms and lemon onto 12 skewers.
3 Cook skewers, on heated oiled grill plate (or grill or barbecue) until browned all over and cooked through, brushing skewers with juice mixture while cooking.

on the table in 35 minutes
serves 4 **per serving** 12.8g total fat (2.0g saturated fat); 1170kJ (280 cal); 4.5g carbohydrate; 34.2g protein; 7.7g fibre
tip soak 12 bamboo skewers in water for about 30 minutes before use to prevent splintering and scorching.

Chicken with mango salsa

4 breast fillets (800g)
mango salsa
120g spinach, shredded finely
1 medium red onion (170g), chopped finely
1 medium mango (430g), chopped finely
1 tablespoon coarsely chopped fresh mint
¼ cup (20g) flaked parmesan cheese
¼ cup (60ml) sweet chilli sauce

1 Cook chicken, on heated oiled grill plate (or grill or barbecue) until browned all over and cooked through.
2 Meanwhile, make mango salsa.
3 Serve chicken topped with mango salsa.
mango salsa place ingredients in medium bowl; toss gently to combine.

on the table in 25 minutes
serves 4 **per serving** 6.6g total fat (2.2g saturated fat); 1375kJ (329 cal); 15.7g carbohydrate; 49.6g protein; 2.7g fibre

Harissa chicken with couscous salad

4 breast fillets (800g), sliced thickly
2 tablespoons harissa
2 teaspoons finely grated lemon rind
couscous salad
1½ cups (375ml) chicken stock
2 teaspoons ground coriander
1½ cups (300g) couscous
1 medium red capsicum (200g), chopped finely
1 medium brown onion (150g), chopped finely
3 green onions, sliced thinly
½ cup firmly packed fresh coriander leaves
⅓ cup (80ml) lemon juice
1 tablespoon olive oil

1 Combine chicken, harissa and rind in medium bowl.
2 Make couscous salad.
3 Meanwhile, cook chicken mixture on heated oiled grill plate (or grill or barbecue) until browned all over and cooked through.
4 Serve chicken on couscous salad.
couscous salad bring stock and ground coriander to a boil in medium saucepan. Remove from heat; stir in couscous. Cover; stand about 5 minutes or until liquid is absorbed, fluffing occasionally with fork. Add remaining ingredients; toss gently to combine.

on the table in 30 minutes
serves 4 **per serving** 10.5g total fat (2.2g saturated fat); 2470kJ (591 cal); 64.2g carbohydrate; 57.4g protein; 2.7g fibre
tip harissa, a North African paste made from dried red chillies, garlic, olive oil and caraway seeds, can be used as a rub for meat, an ingredient in sauces and dressings, or eaten on its own, as a condiment. It is available ready-made from Middle-Eastern food shops and some supermarkets.

Chicken skewers with chilli garlic mayonnaise

500g thigh fillets
1 teaspoon finely grated lime rind
¼ cup (60ml) lime juice
1 tablespoon olive oil
chilli garlic mayonnaise
1 egg yolk
2 cloves garlic, crushed
2 tablespoons lime juice
2 tablespoons sweet chilli sauce
1 cup (250ml) peanut oil
1 tablespoon coarsely chopped fresh coriander

1 Cut chicken into 3cm pieces; thread onto eight skewers. Combine rind, juice and oil in shallow dish, add skewers; turn to coat well. Cover; stand 10 minutes.
2 Meanwhile, make chilli garlic mayonnaise.
3 Cook skewers, on heated oiled grill plate (or grill or barbecue) until browned all over and cooked through, brushing skewers with marinade while cooking.
4 Serve skewers with mayonnaise.
chilli garlic mayonnaise blend or process egg yolk, garlic, juice and sauce until smooth. With motor operating, gradually add the oil in a thin stream; blend until thick. Stir in coriander.

on the table in 35 minutes
serves 4 **per serving** 72.2g total fat (14.2g saturated fat); 3127kJ (748 cal); 2.5g carbohydrate; 24.5g protein; 0.8g fibre
tip soak 8 bamboo skewers in water for about 30 minutes before use to prevent splintering and scorching.

Citrus chicken with char-grilled orange and corn

4 breast fillets (800g)
⅔ cup (160ml) lemon juice
¾ cup (180ml) orange juice
3 cloves garlic, crushed
1 tablespoon finely chopped fresh oregano
1 teaspoon ground cumin
1 fresh small red thai chilli, chopped finely
1 tablespoon olive oil
3 trimmed corn cobs (750g), quartered
1 large orange (300g), unpeeled, cut into 8 wedges
8 green onions, cut into 8cm lengths

1 Combine chicken, juices, garlic, oregano, cumin, chilli and oil in medium bowl. Stand 10 minutes
2 Drain chicken; reserve marinade. Cook chicken on heated oiled grill plate (or grill or barbecue) until browned all over and cooked through.
3 Cook corn, orange and onion on heated oiled grill plate until tender.
4 Place reserved marinade in small saucepan; bring to a boil. Reduce heat, simmer, uncovered, 2 minutes.
5 Serve chicken with corn, orange and onion, drizzled with marinade.

on the table in 35 minutes
serves 4 **per serving** 11.1g total fat (2.0g saturated fat); 1920kJ (459 cal); 32.5g carbohydrate; 52.5g protein; 8.2g fibre

Chicken with lentil salsa

12 tenderloins (900g)
2 teaspoons ground cumin
2 teaspoons ground coriander
1 teaspoon ground turmeric
1½ cups (300g) red lentils
1 clove garlic, crushed
1 fresh small red thai chilli, chopped finely
1 lebanese cucumber (130g), seeded, chopped finely
1 medium red capsicum (200g), chopped finely
¼ cup (60ml) lemon juice
2 teaspoons peanut oil
2 tablespoons coarsely chopped fresh coriander
2 limes, cut into wedges

1 Combine chicken and spices in medium bowl.
2 Cook lentils in large saucepan of boiling water, uncovered, until just tender; drain. Rinse under cold water; drain. Place lentils in large bowl with garlic, chilli, cucumber, capsicum, juice, oil and fresh coriander.
3 Cook chicken on heated oiled grill plate (or grill or barbecue) until browned all over and cooked through. Cook limes on same grill plate until browned both sides.
4 Serve chicken with lentil salsa and lime wedges.

on the table in 25 minutes
serves 4 **per serving** 9.1g total fat (2.0g saturated fat); 2157kJ (516 cal); 31.6g carbohydrate; 70.2g protein; 11.7g fibre

Chicken ratatouille

4 breast fillets (800g)
1 tablespoon olive oil
1 medium brown onion (150g), chopped finely
1 medium yellow capsicum (200g), chopped coarsely
1 medium red capsicum (200g), chopped coarsely
1 medium eggplant (300g), chopped coarsely
1 tablespoon tomato paste
3 small zucchini (270g), chopped coarsely
700g jar tomato pasta sauce
½ cup (125ml) chicken stock
1 cup coarsely chopped fresh basil
8 small fresh basil leaves

1 Using meat mallet, gently pound chicken between sheets of plastic wrap until 2cm thick. Cook chicken on heated oiled grill plate (or grill or barbecue) until browned all over and cooked through.
2 Heat oil in medium saucepan; cook onion, stirring, until onion softens. Add capsicums, eggplant and paste; cook, stirring, 2 minutes. Add zucchini; cook, stirring, 2 minutes. Add sauce and stock; bring to a boil. Reduce heat, simmer, covered, 8 minutes, stirring occasionally. Uncover; cook 3 minutes. Remove from heat; stir in chopped basil.
3 Serve chicken with ratatouille; top with whole basil leaves.

on the table in 25 minutes
serves 4 **per serving** 11.1g total fat (2.1g saturated fat); 1781kJ (426 cal); 25.3g carbohydrate; 51.8g protein; 7.8g fibre

Yakitori chicken

4 breast fillets (800g)
¼ cup (60ml) mirin
½ cup (125ml) light soy sauce
2cm piece fresh ginger (10g), grated
2 cloves garlic, crushed
¼ teaspoon ground black pepper
1 tablespoon white sugar

1 Cut chicken into 2cm pieces. Combine chicken with remaining ingredients in large bowl; stand 10 minutes.
2 Drain chicken over small bowl; reserve marinade. Thread chicken onto 12 skewers.
3 Cook skewers on heated oiled grill plate (or grill or barbecue) until browned all over and cooked through, brushing with reserved marinade occasionally during cooking.

on the table in 35 minutes
serves 4 **per serving** 4.7g total fat (1.2g saturated fat); 1099kJ (263 cal); 5.3g carbohydrate; 47.2g protein; 0.2g fibre
tips mirin is a somewhat sweet rice wine used in many Asian, especially Japanese, dishes. You can substitute sherry or sweet white wine for mirin, if you prefer. Soak 12 bamboo skewers in water for about 30 minutes before use to prevent splintering and scorching during cooking.

Cajun chicken with pineapple salsa

8 thigh fillets (880g)
1 tablespoon sweet paprika
1 teaspoon cayenne pepper
2 teaspoons garlic powder
2 teaspoons dried oregano
1 tablespoon olive oil
pineapple salsa
4 rashers rindless bacon (250g)
1 small pineapple (800g), chopped finely
1 fresh small red thai chilli, chopped finely
¼ cup coarsely chopped fresh flat-leaf parsley
1 medium red capsicum (200g), chopped coarsely
¼ cup (60ml) lime juice
1 teaspoon olive oil

1 Combine chicken, spices, oregano and oil in large bowl.
2 Make pineapple salsa.
3 Cook chicken mixture on heated oiled grill plate (or grill or barbecue) until browned all over and cooked through.
4 Serve chicken with salsa and lemon wedges, if desired.
pineapple salsa cook bacon on heated oiled flat plate until crisp; drain then chop coarsely. Place bacon in medium bowl with remaining ingredients; toss gently to combine.

on the table in 30 minutes
serves 4 per serving 31.1g total fat (9.7g saturated fat); 2299kJ (550 cal); 10.5g carbohydrate; 56.4g protein; 2.9g fibre

Portuguese-style chicken thighs

2 teaspoons cracked black pepper
1 teaspoon dried oregano
2 fresh small red thai chillies, chopped finely
½ teaspoon hot paprika
1 clove garlic, crushed
¼ cup (60ml) red wine vinegar
¼ cup (60ml) olive oil
6 thigh fillets (660g), halved

1 Combine pepper, oregano, chilli, paprika, garlic, vinegar and oil in medium bowl. Reserve about a quarter of the spicy mixture in small jug; use hands to rub remaining spicy mixture onto chicken pieces.
2 Cook chicken on heated oiled grill plate (or grill or barbecue) until browned all over and cooked through.
3 Serve chicken drizzled with reserved spicy mixture.

on the table in 25 minutes
serves 4 **per serving** 25.7g total fat (5.6g saturated fat); 1488kJ (356 cal); 1.0g carbohydrate; 31.0g protein; 0.4g fibre

Lemon chicken with baby spinach salad

12 tenderloins (900g)
2 tablespoons lemon juice
1 tablespoon fresh thyme leaves
½ cup (125ml) olive oil
100g baby spinach leaves
1 small red onion (100g), chopped finely
250g cherry tomatoes, halved
80g snow pea sprouts
⅓ cup (80ml) red wine vinegar
½ teaspoon dijon mustard

1 Using meat mallet, gently pound chicken between sheets of plastic.
2 Combine chicken, juice, thyme and 2 tablespoons of the oil in large bowl.
3 Cook chicken mixture on heated oiled grill plate (or grill or barbecue) until browned all over and cooked through.
4 Place spinach, onion, tomato and sprouts in large bowl. Combine remaining oil, vinegar and mustard in screw-top jar; shake well. Drizzle dressing over salad; toss gently to combine.
5 Serve salad topped with chicken.

on the table in 35 minutes
serves 4 **per serving** 34.0g total fat (5.4g saturated fat); 2328kJ (557 cal); 7.9g carbohydrate; 54.0g protein; 2.9g fibre

Salt and pepper chicken skewers on baby buk choy

800g thigh fillets, chopped coarsely
1 teaspoon sichuan peppercorns, crushed
½ teaspoon five-spice powder
2 teaspoons sea salt
1 teaspoon sesame oil
600g baby buk choy, quartered
1 tablespoon oyster sauce
1 teaspoon soy sauce
1 tablespoon chopped fresh coriander

1 Thread chicken onto 12 skewers. Combine peppercorns, five-spice and salt in small bowl; sprinkle mixture over chicken, then press in firmly.
2 Cook skewers, on heated oiled grill plate (or grill or barbecue) until browned all over and cooked through.
3 Meanwhile, heat oil in wok; stir-fry buk choy with combined sauces until just wilted.
4 Divide buk choy among serving plates; top with chicken skewers. Serve sprinkled with coriander.

on the table in 35 minutes
serves 4 **per serving** 16.0g total fat (4.6g saturated fat); 1320kJ (316 cal); 3.2g carbohydrate; 39.2g protein; 2.1g fibre
tip soak 12 bamboo skewers in water for about 30 minutes before use to prevent splintering and scorching during cooking.

Chicken with red pesto pasta

4 breast fillets (800g)
¼ cup (75g) bottled red pesto
375g spaghetti
1 cup (70g) stale breadcrumbs
⅓ cup finely chopped fresh chives
2 teaspoons wholegrain mustard
½ cup (125ml) chicken stock

1 Coat chicken with half the pesto.
2 Cook spaghetti in large saucepan of boiling water, uncovered, until just tender; drain. Rinse under cold water; drain.
3 Meanwhile, cook chicken on heated oiled grill plate (or grill or barbecue) until browned all over and cooked through. Cover loosely to keep warm.
4 Heat oiled large saucepan; cook breadcrumbs, stirring, until browned. Stir in spaghetti with remaining pesto, chives, mustard and stock; cook, stirring, until hot.
5 Serve spaghetti with sliced chicken, and tomato wedges, if desired.

on the table in 35 minutes
serves 4 **per serving** 14.0g total fat (3.2g saturated fat); 2926kJ (700 cal); 78.6g carbohydrate; 60.5g protein; 6.1g fibre
tip we used sun-dried capsicum pesto for this recipe, but any bottled "red" pesto, such as tomato, could be used.

Balsamic chicken with rosemary potatoes

6 thigh fillets (660g)
¼ cup (60ml) balsamic vinegar
¼ cup (60ml) olive oil
2 tablespoons fresh rosemary leaves
700g potatoes, cut into 2cm pieces
6 medium zucchini (720g), sliced thickly

1 Combine chicken, vinegar, 2 tablespoons of the oil and half of the rosemary in medium bowl.
2 Boil, steam or microwave potato until just tender; drain.
3 Drain chicken; reserve marinade. Cook chicken on heated oiled grill plate (or grill or barbecue) until browned all over and cooked through.
4 Toss potato in medium bowl with remaining rosemary and remaining oil. Cook potato, on heated oiled flat plate, uncovered, until tender.
5 Cook zucchini on heated oiled flat plate, uncovered, brushing with reserved marinade, until browned lightly.
6 Cut chicken pieces in half; serve with potato and zucchini.

on the table in 30 minutes
serves 4 **per serving** 26.3g total fat (5.6g saturated fat); 2077kJ (497 cal); 28.8g carbohydrate; 37.1g protein; 5.7g fibre

Chicken skewers with papaya salsa

12 tenderloins (900g)
1 small papaya (650g), seeded, chopped finely
4 green onions, sliced thinly
1 lebanese cucumber (130g), seeded, chopped coarsely
½ cup coarsely chopped fresh mint
2cm piece fresh ginger (10g), grated
1 tablespoon sweet chilli sauce
2 tablespoons lime juice

1 Thread chicken onto 12 skewers.
2 Cook skewers on heated oiled grill plate (or grill or barbecue) until browned all over and cooked through.
3 Meanwhile, combine papaya, onion, cucumber, mint, ginger, sauce and juice in small bowl.
4 Serve skewers topped with salsa.

on the table in 25 minutes
serves 4 **per serving** 5.6g total fat (1.4g saturated fat); 1258kJ (301 cal); 10.2g carbohydrate; 52.0g protein; 3.8g fibre
tips soak 12 bamboo skewers in water for about 30 minutes before use to prevent splintering and scorching during cooking. You can substitute mango for the papaya if you prefer.

Chilli chicken with couscous

4 breast fillets (800g)
⅓ cup (80ml) prepared moroccan marinade
2 cups (500ml) vegetable stock
2 cups (400g) couscous
20g butter
1 small red onion (100g), sliced thinly
2 fresh small red thai chillies, chopped finely
½ cup (110g) coarsely chopped seeded prunes
⅓ cup (45g) slivered almonds, toasted
½ cup coarsely chopped fresh mint
¼ cup (45g) finely chopped preserved lemon

1 Combine chicken and marinade in large bowl; stand 10 minutes.
2 Meanwhile, bring stock to a boil in medium saucepan. Remove
from heat; stir in couscous and butter. Cover; stand 5 minutes or
until liquid is absorbed, fluffing couscous with fork occasionally.
Stir in remaining ingredients.
3 Cook chicken mixture on heated oiled grill plate (or grill or barbecue)
until browned all over and cooked through; slice thickly.
4 Serve chicken on couscous.

on the table in 30 minutes
serves 4 **per serving** 23.5g total fat (5.4g saturated fat); 3557kJ
(851 cal); 90.6g carbohydrate; 64.2g protein; 7.5g fibre
tips moroccan marinade is a bottled blend of garlic, capsicum, chilli,
lemon and various spices, and can be found at your local supermarket.
Preserved lemons – salted lemons preserved in a mixture of olive oil and
lemon juice – are a North African specialty, usually added to casseroles
and tagines to impart a salty-sour acidic flavour. They're available from
good food shops and delicatessens. Rinse preserved lemons well under
cold water, discard flesh then finely chop the rind.

Five-spice chicken

750g tenderloins
1 teaspoon peanut oil
1 ½ teaspoons five-spice powder
2 cloves garlic, crushed
250g hokkien noodles
300g baby corn
500g asparagus, trimmed
1 medium red capsicum (200g), sliced thinly
¼ cup chopped fresh flat-leaf parsley

1 Combine chicken, oil, five-spice and garlic in medium bowl.
2 Cook chicken mixture on heated oiled grill plate (or grill or barbecue) until browned all over and cooked through.
3 Place noodles in medium heatproof bowl, cover with boiling water, separate with fork; drain.
4 Cut baby corn in half. Chop asparagus into same-sized pieces as halved corn. Stir-fry corn, asparagus and capsicum in heated oiled wok until just tender; add noodles.
5 Stir parsley into vegetables off the heat, then divide mixture among serving dishes; top with chicken.

on the table in 35 minutes
serves 4 **per serving** 6.8g total fat (1.4g saturated fat); 1689kJ (404 cal); 30.7g carbohydrate; 51.0g protein; 6.7g fibre

Chicken wings and green mango salad

16 wings (1.5kg)
10cm stick (20g) fresh lemon grass, chopped finely
1 long green chilli, chopped finely
3 cloves garlic, crushed
10 fresh kaffir lime leaves, shredded finely
2 small green mangoes (600g)
1 large carrot (180g)
1 lebanese cucumber (130g)
1 medium red capsicum (200g), sliced thinly
2 green onions, sliced thinly
sweet and sour dressing
2 tablespoons fish sauce
2 tablespoons lime juice
2 tablespoons grated palm sugar
1 tablespoon white vinegar
1 tablespoon water

1 Make sweet and sour dressing.
2 Combine chicken, lemon grass, chilli, garlic, about half of the lime leaves and 2 tablespoons of the dressing in medium bowl. Stand 10 minutes.
3 Meanwhile, use vegetable peeler to finely slice mangoes, carrot and cucumber into ribbons. Place in medium bowl with capsicum, remaining lime leaves and remaining dressing; toss gently to combine.
4 Drain chicken; discard marinade. Cook chicken mixture on heated oiled grill plate (or grill or barbecue) until browned all over and cooked through.
5 Serve chicken with salad, sprinkled with onion.
sweet and sour dressing place ingredients in screw-top jar; shake well.

on the table in 35 minutes
serves 4 **per serving** 13.0g total fat (4.1g saturated fat); 1922kJ (459 cal); 25.3g carbohydrate; 57.4g protein; 4.3g fibre

Tandoori chicken salad

750g tenderloins
½ cup (140g) yogurt
1½ tablespoons tandoori paste
¾ cup (200g) yogurt, extra
¼ cup (60ml) mint sauce
250g mesclun
4 large egg tomatoes (360g), chopped
2 lebanese cucumbers (260g), chopped

1 Combine chicken, yogurt and paste in large bowl.
2 Cook chicken mixture on heated oiled grill plate (or grill or barbecue) until browned all over and cooked through.
3 Combine extra yogurt and sauce in small bowl.
4 Divide mesclun among serving plates, top with tomato, cucumber and chicken. Serve drizzled with yogurt mint sauce.

on the table in 20 minutes
serves 4 **per serving** 16.3g total fat (5.3g saturated fat); 1634kJ (390 cal); 11.9g carbohydrate; 46.9g protein; 4.4g fibre

Thai chicken and rice

2 cups (400g) long-grain white rice
1 cup firmly packed fresh mint leaves
⅓ cup (80ml) sweet chilli sauce
1 tablespoon fish sauce
1 tablespoon soy sauce
½ cup (125ml) lime juice
2cm piece fresh ginger (10g), grated
¼ cup coarsely chopped fresh lemon grass
4 breast fillets (800g)
1 small red capsicum (150g), chopped finely

1 Cook rice in large saucepan of boiling water, uncovered, until just tender; drain.
2 Meanwhile, reserve 2 tablespoons of the mint; blend or process remaining mint with sauces, juice, ginger and lemon grass until smooth.
3 Cook chicken on heated oiled grill plate (or grill or barbecue) until browned all over and cooked through.
4 Toss capsicum through cooked rice. Divide among serving plates; top with chicken. Drizzle with sauce; sprinkle with reserved coarsely chopped mint.

on the table in 20 minutes
serves 4 **per serving** 5.4g total fat (1.3g saturated fat); 2253kJ (539 cal); 66.9g carbohydrate; 52.6g protein; 3.3g fibre

Chicken on warm lentil salad

4 breast fillets (800g)
2 teaspoons olive oil
1 small brown onion (80g), chopped finely
2 rashers rindless bacon (125g), chopped finely
2 cloves garlic, crushed
¼ cup (60ml) dry white wine
¼ cup (60ml) chicken stock
2 x 400g cans lentils, rinsed, drained
250g cherry tomatoes, quartered
½ cup fresh flat-leaf parsley leaves

1 Cut each breast in half horizontally. Cook on heated oiled grill plate (or grill or barbecue) until browned both sides and cooked through. Cover to keep warm.
2 Heat oil in medium saucepan; cook onion, bacon and garlic, stirring, until bacon is browned and onion is soft.
3 Add wine; cook until wine is almost evaporated. Add stock and lentils; cook until lentils are hot and stock is reduced by half. Remove from heat; add tomatoes and parsley, stir gently to combine.
4 Serve chicken with lentil salad.

on the table in 25 minutes
serves 4 **per serving** 12.8g total fat (3.5g saturated fat); 1781kJ (426 cal); 12.0g carbohydrate; 60.2g protein; 5.4g fibre

Minted chutney chicken

4 breast fillets (800g)
2 tablespoons olive oil
2 teaspoons finely grated lemon rind
¼ cup lemon juice (60ml)
2 tablespoons mango chutney
2 tablespoons chopped fresh mint

1 Combine chicken, oil, rind, juice, chutney and mint in medium bowl.
Stand 10 minutes.
2 Drain chicken; reserve marinade. Cook chicken mixture on heated oiled
grill plate (or grill or barbecue) until browned all over and cooked through,
brushing occasionally with reserved marinade.

on the table in 35 minutes
serves 4 **per serving** 13.8g total fat (2.5g saturated fat); 1388kJ
(332 cal); 5.9g carbohydrate; 45.4g protein; 0.5g fibre

Chicken kofta with red capsicum and walnut sauce

700g mince
1 large brown onion (200g), chopped finely
1½ cups (110g) stale breadcrumbs
1 egg
¼ cup finely chopped fresh coriander
3 teaspoons ground cumin
2 teaspoons ground allspice
6 pitta pocket bread, halved
100g baby rocket leaves
red capsicum and walnut sauce
2 medium red capsicums (400g)
⅓ cup (35g) toasted walnuts
2 tablespoons stale breadcrumbs
2 tablespoons lemon juice
1 teaspoon sambal oelek
½ teaspoon ground cumin
2 tablespoons olive oil

1 Using hand, combine chicken, onion, breadcrumbs, egg, coriander and spices in large bowl; shape ¼ cups of the mixture around each of 12 skewers to form slightly flattened sausage shapes. Place kofta on tray. Cover; refrigerate 10 minutes.
2 Meanwhile, make red capsicum and walnut sauce.
3 Cook kofta on heated oiled grill plate (or grill or barbecue) until browned all over and cooked through.
4 Serve kofta with warm pitta bread, rocket and sauce.
red capsicum and walnut sauce quarter capsicums; discard seeds and membranes. Cook on heated oiled grill plate (or grill or barbecue), skin-side down until skin blisters and blackens. Cover pieces with plastic wrap or paper for 5 minutes; peel away skin. Blend or process capsicum with remaining ingredients until smooth.

on the table in 35 minutes
serves 4 **per serving** 28.0g total fat (4.7g saturated fat); 3486kJ (834 cal); 87.8g carbohydrate; 57.0g protein; 1.4g fibre
tip soak 12 bamboo skewers in water for about 30 minutes before use to prevent splintering and scorching.

Chicken skewers with chilli and lime sauce

⅓ cup (80ml) sweet chilli sauce
2 tablespoons fish sauce
2 tablespoons lime juice
6 thigh fillets (660g), halved lengthways
1 green onion, sliced thinly

1 Combine sauces and juice in small bowl; reserve half of the sauce in small serving bowl.
2 Thread chicken onto 12 skewers lengthways; brush chicken with remaining sauce. Cook skewers on heated oiled grill plate (or grill or barbecue) until browned all over and cooked through.
3 Add onion to reserved sauce; serve sauce with skewers.

on the table in 25 minutes
serves 4 **per serving** 12.0g total fat (3.6g saturated fat); 1083kJ (259 cal); 5.6g carbohydrate; 32.2g protein; 0.4g fibre
tip soak 12 bamboo skewers in water for about 30 minutes before use to prevent splintering and scorching.

Chicken with buk choy and flat mushrooms

2 tablespoons honey
⅓ cup (80ml) soy sauce
2 tablespoons dry sherry
1 teaspoon five-spice powder
4cm piece fresh ginger (20g), grated
1 tablespoon peanut oil
4 breast fillets (800g)
4 flat mushrooms (360g)
500g baby buk choy, quartered lengthways
1 cup (250ml) chicken stock
2 teaspoons cornflour
2 tablespoons water

1 Combine honey, sauce, sherry, five-spice, ginger and oil in small jug.
2 Combine chicken and half of the honey mixture in medium bowl. Cover; refrigerate 10 minutes.
3 Meanwhile, cook mushrooms and buk choy on heated oiled grill plate (or grill or barbecue) until just tender; cover to keep warm.
4 Cook drained chicken on same oiled grill plate (or grill or barbecue) until browned all over and cooked through; slice thickly.
5 Combine remaining honey mixture in small saucepan with stock; bring to a boil. Stir in blended cornflour and water; cook, stirring, until sauce boils and thickens slightly.
6 Divide mushrooms and buk choy among serving plates; top with chicken, drizzle with sauce.

on the table in 35 minutes
serves 4 **per serving** 9.6g total fat (2.2g saturated fat); 1593kJ (381 cal); 16.2g carbohydrate; 51.7g protein; 4.0g fibre

Chicken with warm tomato salad

4 breast fillets (800g)
2 tablespoons lime juice
¼ cup (60ml) sweet chilli sauce
2 cloves garlic, crushed
4 fresh kaffir lime leaves, shredded
20g butter
2 medium brown onions (300g), sliced thickly
2 tablespoons red wine vinegar
¼ cup (55g) white sugar
2 tablespoons sweet chilli sauce, extra
¼ cup (60ml) water
¼ cup (60ml) orange juice
6 medium egg tomatoes (450g), cut into wedges
1 tablespoon bottled jalapeño chillies, chopped coarsely
3 green onions, sliced thickly

1 Combine chicken, juice, sauce, garlic and lime leaves in large bowl.
2 Heat butter in large saucepan; cook brown onion, stirring, until just softened. Add vinegar and sugar; cook, stirring, 2 minutes. Stir in extra sauce, the water and juice; add tomato and chilli, stir until heated through.
3 Cook drained chicken, on heated oiled grill plate (or grill or barbecue) until browned all over and cooked through. Slice thickly.
4 Serve chicken on warm tomato salad; top with green onion.

on the table in 30 minutes
serves 4 **per serving** 9.7g total fat (4.0g saturated fat); 1668kJ (399 cal); 27.2g carbohydrate; 48.1g protein; 4.3g fibre

Herbed chicken skewers with roasted pecans

1kg breast fillets, chopped
½ cup finely chopped fresh chives
⅓ cup finely chopped fresh oregano
¼ cup finely chopped fresh marjoram
4 cloves garlic, crushed
1 tablespoon lemon pepper seasoning
2 tablespoons chicken stock
¼ cup (30g) chopped pecans, roasted

1 Thread chicken onto 12 skewers.
2 Combine herbs, garlic, seasoning and stock in shallow dish; add skewers.
3 Cook skewers on heated oiled grill plate (or grill or barbecue) until browned all over and cooked through.
4 Serve sprinkled with pecans.

on the table in 35 minutes
serves 6 **per serving** 7.5g total fat (1.2g saturated fat); 949kJ (227 cal); 0.6g carbohydrate; 38.4g protein; 0.9g fibre
tip soak 12 bamboo skewers in water for about 30 minutes before use to prevent splintering and scorching.

Chicken and pickled cucumber pitta

1 medium green cucumber (170g)
1 tablespoon cider vinegar
2 teaspoons white sugar
1 fresh small red thai chilli, chopped finely
1 teaspoon soy sauce
2 breast fillets (400g)
1 small butter lettuce
4 pitta pocket bread

1 Slice cucumber into long, thin strips with a vegetable peeler. Place in medium bowl with vinegar, sugar, chilli and sauce; stand 10 minutes.
2 Meanwhile, cook chicken on heated oiled grill plate (or grill or barbecue) until browned all over and cooked through; slice thinly.
3 Serve chicken, pickled cucumber and lettuce in pittas.

on the table in 35 minutes
serves 4 **per serving** 4.3g total fat (0.8g saturated fat); 1450kJ (347 cal); 43.6g carbohydrate; 31.0g protein; 3.4g fibre

Mustard chicken with grilled citrus

4 breast fillets (800g)
2 tablespoons olive oil
2 teaspoons dijon mustard
2 tablespoons fresh lemon thyme leaves
2 medium lemons (280g)
2 limes
¼ cup (60g) dijon mustard, extra

1 Combine chicken, oil, mustard and half the thyme in medium bowl.
Stand 10 minutes.
2 Drain chicken; reserve marinade. Cook chicken mixture on heated oiled grill plate (or grill or barbecue) until browned all over and cooked through, brushing with reserved marinade during cooking. Cover to keep warm.
Cut into pieces.
3 Cut each lemon into six wedges and each lime into four wedges; cook on same heated oiled grill plate until browned both sides.
4 Combine extra mustard and remaining thyme in small bowl.
5 Serve chicken with citrus wedges and thyme mustard.

on the table in 35 minutes
serves 4 **per serving** 14.4g total fat (2.5g saturated fat); 1379kJ (330 cal); 2.3g carbohydrate; 46.7g protein; 2.4g fibre

Chicken tikka with cucumber-mint raita

1kg breast fillets
½ cup (150g) tikka paste
cucumber-mint raita
¾ cup (200g) yogurt
1 lebanese cucumber (130g), peeled, seeded, chopped finely
2 tablespoons finely chopped fresh mint
1 teaspoon ground cumin

1 Combine chicken and paste in large bowl.
2 Make cucumber-mint raita.
3 Cook chicken mixture on heated oiled grill plate (or grill or barbecue) until browned all over and cooked through; slice thinly.
4 Serve chicken with cucumber-mint raita on a bed of finely shredded cabbage, if desired.
cucumber-mint raita combine ingredients in small bowl.

on the table in 25 minutes
serves 6 **per serving** 12.8g total fat (2.5g saturated fat); 1254kJ (300 cal); 4.0g carbohydrate; 40.7g protein; 2.9g fibre

Sumac and paprika-spiced chicken with herb salad

8 tenderloins (600g)
2 cloves garlic, crushed
2 teaspoons sweet paprika
2 tablespoons sumac
2 teaspoons finely chopped fresh oregano
2 tablespoons water
1 teaspoon vegetable oil
2½ cups coarsely chopped fresh flat-leaf parsley
1 cup coarsely chopped fresh coriander
½ cup coarsely chopped fresh mint
4 medium tomatoes (600g), chopped coarsely
1 medium red onion (170g), chopped coarsely
⅓ cup (80ml) lemon juice
1 tablespoon olive oil

1 Thread chicken onto skewers. Using fingers, rub combined garlic, paprika, sumac, oregano, the water and vegetable oil all over chicken.
2 Cook skewers on heated oiled grill plate (or grill or barbecue) until browned all over and cooked through.
3 Place herbs, tomato and onion in medium bowl with juice and olive oil; toss gently to combine. Serve skewers with herb salad.

on the table in 35 minutes
serves 4 **per serving** 9.6g total fat (1.7g saturated fat); 1145kJ (274 cal); 6.6g carbohydrate; 37.5g protein; 5.2g fibre
tip soak 8 bamboo skewers in water for about 30 minutes before use to prevent splintering and scorching during cooking.

salads

Greek salad with smoked chicken

1 small red onion (100g), sliced thinly
200g fetta cheese, crumbled
250g grape tomatoes
400g smoked breast, sliced thinly
200g baby spinach leaves
⅔ cup (110g) seeded kalamata olives
1 medium red capsicum (200g), sliced thinly
dressing
⅓ cup (80ml) olive oil
¼ cup (60ml) lemon juice
1 clove garlic, crushed

1 Combine onion, cheese, tomatoes, chicken, spinach, olives and capsicum in large bowl.
2 Make dressing; drizzle over salad. Toss gently to combine.
dressing place ingredients in screw-top jar; shake well.

on the table in 20 minutes
serves 4 **per serving** 37.5g total fat (12.3g saturated fat); 2228kJ (533 cal); 11.5g carbohydrate; 36.4g protein; 3.6g fibre
tip smoked chicken breast may be slightly pink, like bacon and ham, but this does not mean it is undercooked.

Honey chilli chicken salad

3 breast fillets (600g), sliced thinly
¼ cup (90g) honey
4 fresh small red thai chillies, sliced thinly
4cm piece fresh ginger (20g), grated
500g asparagus, trimmed
2 tablespoons peanut oil
4 green onions, sliced thinly
1 medium green capsicum (200g), sliced thinly
1 medium yellow capsicum (200g), sliced thinly
1 medium carrot (120g), sliced thinly
150g wombok, shredded finely
⅓ cup (80ml) lime juice

1 Combine chicken, honey, chilli and ginger in medium bowl.
2 Cut asparagus spears in half; boil, steam or microwave until just tender. Rinse immediately under cold water; drain.
3 Heat half of the oil in large frying pan; cook chicken, in batches, until browned all over and cooked through.
4 Place chicken and asparagus in large bowl with onion, capsicums, carrot, wombok, juice and remaining oil; toss gently to combine.

on the table in 25 minutes
serves 4 **per serving** 12.8g total fat (2.5g saturated fat); 1572kJ (376 cal); 24.5g carbohydrate; 38.4g protein; 3.7g fibre
tip you will need two bunches of asparagus and a quarter of a medium wombok for this recipe.

American chicken salad

1½ cups (375ml) chicken stock
½ cup (125ml) water
3 breast fillets (600g)
1 small baguette (165g), sliced thinly
2 tablespoons vegetable oil
¾ cup (225g) mayonnaise
½ cup (120g) sour cream
2 tablespoons lemon juice
3 trimmed celery stalks (300g), sliced thinly
1 medium white onion (150g), chopped finely
⅔ cup (110g) thinly sliced dill pickles
2 tablespoons finely chopped fresh flat-leaf parsley
1 tablespoon finely chopped fresh tarragon
1 large butter lettuce, leaves separated

1 Combine stock and the water in medium shallow saucepan; bring to a boil. Add chicken; simmer, loosely covered, about 10 minutes, turning once, until chicken is cooked through. Remove chicken from pan; stand 10 minutes before slicing.
2 Meanwhile, brush bread slices with oil; toast until golden.
3 Whisk mayonnaise, cream and juice in small bowl until combined.
4 Place chicken, celery, onion, pickles and herbs in large bowl; toss gently to combine.
5 Serve in lettuce leaves with toasted bread slices, drizzled with mayonnaise mixture.

on the table in 35 minutes
serves 4 **per serving** 15.7g total fat (3.4g saturated fat); 1639kJ (392 cal); 7.1g carbohydrate; 53.8g protein; 3.8g fibre

Chicken, fennel and orange salad

30g butter
3 breast fillets (600g), sliced thinly
1 large fennel bulb (550g), sliced thinly
½ cup (60g) seeded black olives, quartered
3 green onions, chopped coarsely
2 medium oranges (480g), segmented
80g rocket leaves
dressing
½ cup (125ml) orange juice
2 tablespoons red wine vinegar
2 tablespoons olive oil
½ teaspoon white sugar

1 Heat butter in large frying pan; cook chicken, stirring, until well browned and tender.
2 Make dressing.
3 Place chicken in large bowl with fennel, olives, onion, orange, rocket and dressing; toss gently to combine.
dressing place ingredients in screw-top jar; shake well.

on the table in 25 minutes
serves 4 **per serving** 19.2g total fat (6.3g saturated fat); 1647kJ (394 cal); 16.4g carbohydrate; 36.6g protein; 4.6g fibre

Pesto chicken salad

⅓ cup (90g) bottled basil pesto
2 tablespoons balsamic vinegar
4 breast fillets (800g)
6 medium egg tomatoes (450g), halved
125g baby rocket leaves
1 tablespoon olive oil

1 Combine pesto and vinegar in small bowl.
2 Place chicken and tomato on large tray; brush half of the pesto mixture over both.
3 Cook tomato on heated oiled grill plate (or grill or barbecue) until just softened; remove from plate.
4 Cook chicken on same grill plate until browned all over and cooked through; slice thickly.
5 Place chicken and tomato in large bowl with rocket, oil and remaining pesto mixture; toss gently to combine.

on the table in 20 minutes
serves 4 **per serving** 18.4g total fat (3.8g saturated fat); 1597kJ (382 cal); 3.5g carbohydrate; 49.3g protein; 2.3g fibre
tip you can substitute mixed lettuce leaves for the baby rocket.

Vietnamese chicken salad

3 breast fillets (600g)
1 large carrot (180g)
½ cup (125ml) rice wine vinegar
2 teaspoons salt
2 tablespoons caster sugar
1 medium white onion (150g), sliced thinly
1½ cups (120g) bean sprouts
2 cups (160g) finely shredded savoy cabbage
¼ cup firmly packed fresh vietnamese mint leaves
½ cup firmly packed fresh coriander leaves
1 tablespoon crushed toasted peanuts
2 tablespoons fried shallots
vietnamese dressing
2 tablespoons fish sauce
¼ cup (60ml) water
2 tablespoons caster sugar
2 tablespoons lime juice
1 clove garlic, crushed

1 Place chicken in medium saucepan of boiling water; return to a boil.
Reduce heat, simmer, uncovered, about 10 minutes or until cooked
through. Cool chicken in poaching liquid 10 minutes; discard liquid
(or reserve for another use). Shred chicken coarsely.
2 Meanwhile, cut carrot into matchstick-sized pieces. Combine carrot
with vinegar, salt and sugar in large bowl, cover; stand 5 minutes. Add
onion, cover; stand 5 minutes. Add sprouts, cover; stand 3 minutes.
Drain pickled vegetables; discard liquid.
3 Place chicken and pickled vegetables in large bowl with cabbage
and herbs.
4 Make vietnamese dressing, pour over salad; toss gently to combine.
Sprinkle with nuts and shallots.
vietnamese dressing place ingredients in screw-top jar; shake well.

on the table in 35 minutes
serves 4 **per serving** 5.3g total fat (1.1g saturated fat); 1304kJ (312 cal);
24.5g carbohydrate; 38.4g protein; 4.9g fibre
tip fried shallots provide an extra crunchy finish to a salad, stir-fry or
curry. They can be purchased at all Asian grocery stores; once opened,
they will keep for months if stored in a tightly sealed glass jar.

Honey soy chicken salad

3 breast fillets (600g), sliced thinly
2 tablespoons soy sauce
⅓ cup (115g) honey
1 clove garlic, crushed
4 fresh small red thai chillies, chopped finely
300g snow peas
1 small carrot (70g)
1 tablespoon peanut oil
2 cups (160g) finely shredded savoy cabbage
1 medium yellow capsicum (200g), sliced thinly
1 medium red capsicum (200g), sliced thinly
1 lebanese cucumber (130g), seeded, sliced thinly
4 green onions, sliced thinly
½ cup loosely packed fresh mint leaves
2 tablespoons lime juice
2 teaspoons sesame oil

1 Combine chicken, sauce, honey, garlic and half of the chilli in medium bowl. Cover; refrigerate until required.
2 Meanwhile, boil, steam or microwave snow peas until just tender; drain. Rinse immediately under cold water; drain. Using vegetable peeler, slice carrot into ribbons.
3 Heat peanut oil in large frying pan; cook drained chicken, in batches, until browned and cooked through.
4 Place chicken, snow peas and carrot in large serving bowl with remaining ingredients and remaining chilli; toss gently to combine.

on the table in 35 minutes
serves 4 **per serving** 10.8g total fat (2.1g saturated fat); 1701kJ (407 cal); 31.2g carbohydrate; 39.6g protein; 5.9g fibre
tip you will need about a quarter of a small savoy cabbage for this recipe.

Chicken, turkish bread and haloumi salad

300g prepared mixed vegetable antipasto
500g tenderloins, chopped coarsely
2 tablespoons pine nuts
½ long loaf turkish bread
250g haloumi cheese
200g baby rocket leaves
170g marinated artichoke hearts, drained, quartered
250g cherry tomatoes
¼ cup (60ml) balsamic vinegar

1 Drain antipasto in strainer over small bowl; reserve ⅓ cup of the oil.
Chop antipasto finely.
2 Heat 1 tablespoon of the reserved oil in large frying pan; cook chicken,
in batches, until browned all over and cooked through. Cover to keep
warm. Stir-fry pine nuts in same pan until lightly browned.
3 Preheat grill. Cut bread into 1cm slices; place under grill until browned
both sides.
4 Cut haloumi crossways into 16 slices. Heat 1 tablespoon of the
reserved oil in same pan; cook haloumi, in batches, until browned both sides.
5 Toss antipasto, chicken, bread and haloumi in large bowl with rocket,
artichoke and tomatoes. Drizzle with combined remaining oil and vinegar;
sprinkle with pine nuts.

on the table in 25 minutes
serves 4 **per serving** 29.5g total fat (9.3g saturated fat); 2495kJ
(597 cal); 30.6g carbohydrate; 50.6g protein; 3.5g fibre
tip if there is not enough oil in the mixed vegetable antipasto to make
⅓ cup, add olive oil to make up the required amount.

Chicken and couscous salad

1 tablespoon olive oil
800g tenderloins, chopped coarsely
⅔ cup (160ml) chicken stock
20g butter
⅔ cup (130g) couscous
2 teaspoons finely grated lemon rind
⅓ cup (90g) bottled sun-dried tomato pesto
2 tablespoons lemon juice
250g baby rocket leaves

1 Heat oil in large frying pan; cook chicken, in batches, until browned all over and cooked through.
2 Bring stock to a boil in medium saucepan; stir in butter, couscous and rind. Remove from heat. Cover; stand about 5 minutes or until water is absorbed, fluffing couscous with fork occasionally.
3 Whisk pesto and juice in large bowl. Add couscous, chicken and rocket; toss gently to combine.

on the table in 20 minutes
serves 4 **per serving** 23.0g total fat (6.6g saturated fat); 2236kJ (535 cal); 27.2g carbohydrate; 53.7g protein; 1.8g fibre
tip you can use whatever flavour pesto you prefer as a substitute for the sun-dried tomato variety.

Smoked chicken salad with wild rice

2 cups (400g) wild rice blend
200g seedless red grapes
3 trimmed celery stalks (300g), sliced thinly
½ cup (60g) toasted pecans
350g watercress, trimmed
500g smoked breast, sliced thinly
lime and black pepper dressing
½ cup (125ml) lime juice
½ cup (125ml) olive oil
1 tablespoon caster sugar
¼ teaspoon cracked black pepper

1 Cook rice in large saucepan of boiling water, uncovered, until just tender; drain. Rinse under cold water; drain.
2 Meanwhile, make lime and black pepper dressing.
3 Place rice in large bowl with grapes, celery, nuts and half of the dressing; toss gently to combine.
4 Divide watercress among serving plates; top with rice salad then chicken. Drizzle with remaining dressing.
lime and black pepper dressing place ingredients in screw-top jar; shake well.

on the table in 25 minutes
serves 6 **per serving** 33.9g total fat (5.1g saturated fat); 2851kJ (682 cal); 61.9g carbohydrate; 29.1g protein; 6.4g fibre
tips the wild rice blend we use here is a packaged mixture of white long-grain and dark brown wild rice. Smoked chicken breast may be slightly pink, like bacon and ham, but this does not mean it is undercooked.

Chilli lime chicken salad

2 cups (500ml) water
2 cups (500ml) chicken stock
4 breasts fillets (800g)
1 small red capsicum (150g), sliced thinly
4 trimmed red radishes (60g), sliced thinly
¼ small wombok (175g), shredded coarsely
3 green onions, sliced thinly
1 cup (80g) bean sprouts
½ cup loosely packed fresh coriander leaves
½ cup (75g) toasted salted peanuts
chilli lime dressing
⅓ cup (80ml) lime juice
¼ cup (65g) grated palm sugar
2 fresh small red thai chillies, chopped finely
1 clove garlic, crushed
1 tablespoon fish sauce
¼ cup (60ml) peanut oil

1 Bring the water and stock to a boil in large frying pan. Add chicken; reduce heat, simmer, covered, about 10 minutes or until cooked through. Remove from heat; cool chicken in poaching liquid 10 minutes. Slice chicken thinly.
2 Meanwhile, make chilli lime dressing.
3 Place remaining ingredients and half of the dressing in large bowl; toss gently to combine.
4 Divide salad among serving plates; top with chicken, drizzle with remaining dressing.
chilli lime dressing combine juice, sugar, chilli and garlic in small saucepan. Stir over low heat until sugar dissolves; cool 10 minutes. Whisk in sauce and oil.

on the table in 30 minutes
serves 4 **per serving** 27.8g total fat (4.9g saturated fat); 2341kJ (560 cal); 21.7g carbohydrate; 53.9g protein; 3.8g fibre

Chicken and crunchy noodle salad

3 breast fillets (600g)
500g baby buk choy, shredded coarsely
250g cherry tomatoes, halved
50g fresh shiitake mushrooms, sliced thinly
¼ cup firmly packed fresh coriander leaves
1 cup (80g) bean sprouts
3 green onions, sliced thinly
100g crisp fried noodles
dressing
⅓ cup (80ml) light soy sauce
1 teaspoon sesame oil
2 tablespoons dry sherry

1 Make dressing.
2 Cook chicken, in batches, on heated oiled grill plate (or grill or barbecue) until browned all over and cooked through; slice thinly.
3 Combine buk choy, tomato, mushrooms, coriander, sprouts and onion in large bowl.
4 Add chicken, noodles and dressing to buk choy mixture; toss gently to combine.
dressing place ingredients in screw-top jar; shake well.

on the table in 20 minutes
serves 4 **per serving** 7.2g total fat (2.0g saturated fat); 1158kJ (277 cal); 9.2g carbohydrate; 38.8g protein; 4.7g fibre
tip crisp fried noodles are sold packaged (commonly a 100g packet) already deep-fried and ready to eat. They're sometimes labelled crunchy noodles and are available in two widths – thin and spaghetti-like, or wide and flat like fettuccine.

Pasta and chicken salad

3 breast fillets (600g)
250g penne pasta
1 large red capsicum (350g), chopped coarsely
4 large egg tomatoes (360g), seeded, chopped coarsely
6 green onions, sliced thinly
200g fetta cheese, chopped coarsely
80g baby rocket leaves
vinaigrette
¼ cup (60ml) olive oil
⅓ cup (80ml) red wine vinegar
1 teaspoon dijon mustard
1 teaspoon white sugar

1 Place chicken in medium saucepan, cover with boiling water; return to a boil. Reduce heat, simmer, uncovered, about 10 minutes or until chicken is cooked through. Remove chicken from pan; stand 10 minutes before slicing.
2 Meanwhile, cook pasta in large saucepan of boiling water until just tender; drain. Rinse pasta under cold water; drain.
3 Make vinaigrette.
4 Place chicken and pasta in large bowl with remaining ingredients and vinaigrette; toss gently to combine.
vinaigrette place ingredients in screw-top jar; shake well.

on the table in 35 minutes
serves 4 **per serving** 29.9g total fat (10.6g saturated fat); 2914kJ (697 cal); 51.2g carbohydrate; 52.8g protein; 5.9g fibre

Sesame chicken salad

1.5 litres (6 cups) chicken stock
2 star anise
1 tablespoon light soy sauce
1 teaspoon sesame oil
4 breast fillets (800g)
200g snow peas, halved
100g snow pea sprouts
2 cups (160g) bean sprouts
2 trimmed celery stalks (200g), sliced thinly
4 green onions, sliced yhinly
1 tablespoon sesame seeds, toasted
dressing
2 tablespoons soy sauce
1 tablespoon peanut oil
2 teaspoons sesame oil
1cm piece fresh ginger (5g), grated

1 Combine stock, star anise, sauce and oil in large saucepan; bring to a boil. Add chicken; simmer, loosely covered, about 10 minutes or until chicken is cooked through. Remove chicken from pan; stand 10 minutes before slicing.
2 Meanwhile, add peas to medium saucepan of boiling water; drain immediately. Plunge into bowl of iced water for 2 minutes; drain.
3 Make dressing.
4 Place chicken and peas in large bowl with sprouts, celery, onion and dressing; toss gently to combine. Serve topped with sesame seeds.
dressing place ingredients in screw-top jar; shake well.

on the table in 35 minutes
serves 4 **per serving** 22.5g total fat (5.7g saturated fat); 2002kJ (479 cal); 13.1g carbohydrate; 53.9g protein; 4.9g fibre

Smoked chicken and pear salad

1 small radicchio (100g), torn
1 small mignonette lettuce, torn
200g smoked breast, sliced thinly
1 large pear (330g), sliced thinly
1 medium red onion (170g), sliced thinly
red wine vinaigrette
¼ cup (60ml) red wine vinegar
2 tablespoons balsamic vinegar
¼ cup (60ml) olive oil

1 Make red wine vinaigrette.
2 Place radicchio and mignonette in large bowl with remaining ingredients and vinaigrette; toss gently to combine.
red wine vinaigrette place ingredients in screw-top jar; shake well.

on the table in 20 minutes
serves 4 **per serving** 16.2g total fat (2.6g saturated fat); 957kJ (229 cal); 11.2g carbohydrate; 9.6g protein; 3.8g fibre
tip smoked chicken breast may be slightly pink, like bacon and ham, but this does not mean it is undercooked.

Warm chicken and coriander salad

1 tablespoon peanut oil
¼ cup (35g) slivered almonds
700g thigh fillets, sliced thickly
2 tablespoons finely chopped fresh coriander
1 small red capsicum (150g), chopped coarsely
2 trimmed celery stalks (200g), chopped coarsely
250g cherry tomatoes, halved
1 medium avocado (250g), chopped coarsely
3 green onions, chopped coarsely
1 baby cos lettuce, chopped coarsely
dressing
⅓ cup (100g) mayonnaise
⅓ cup (85g) sour cream
2 tablespoons lemon juice

1 Make dressing.
2 Heat oil in large frying pan; cook nuts, stirring, until browned lightly. Remove from pan.
3 Reheat oil in same pan; cook chicken, stirring, until cooked through. Drain on absorbent paper.
4 Place nuts and chicken in large bowl with coriander, capsicum, celery and dressing. Add tomato, avocado, onion and lettuce; toss gently to combine.
dressing combine ingredients in small bowl.

on the table in 30 minutes
serves 4 **per serving** 48.7g total fat (13.6g saturated fat); 2663kJ (637 cal); 10.8g carbohydrate; 38.0g protein; 4.9g fibre

Sesame chicken noodle salad

3 breast fillets (600g), sliced thinly
1 clove garlic, crushed
2 tablespoons sweet chilli sauce
600g fresh egg noodles
1 medium yellow capsicum (200g)
1 large carrot (180g)
200g watercress, trimmed
1 tablespoon peanut oil
250g asparagus, trimmed, halved
2 teaspoons sesame seeds, toasted
dressing
½ teaspoon sesame oil
¼ cup (60ml) rice vinegar
2 tablespoons soy sauce
1 tablespoon lemon juice
1 green onion, sliced thinly
2 teaspoons white sugar

1 Combine chicken, garlic and chilli sauce in large bowl.
2 Cook noodles in large saucepan of boiling water, uncovered, until just tender; drain.
3 Discard seeds and membranes from capsicum; cut capsicum and carrot into long thin strips.
4 Place noodles, capsicum and carrot in large serving bowl with watercress; toss gently to combine.
5 Heat peanut oil in large frying pan; cook chicken mixture, in batches, until browned and tender. Add asparagus to pan; cook until just tender.
6 Make dressing.
7 Add chicken and asparagus to noodle mixture, drizzle with dressing; toss gently to combine. Sprinkle with seeds.
dressing place ingredients in screw-top jar; shake well.

on the table in 30 minutes
serves 6 **per serving** 8.0g total fat (1.5g saturated fat); 1914kJ (458 cal); 57.6g carbohydrate; 35.4g protein; 5.0g fibre

Smoked chicken salad

400g smoked breast, sliced thinly
200g baby spinach leaves
1 medium yellow capsicum (200g), sliced thinly
1 medium red onion (170g), sliced thinly
1 cup firmly packed fresh purple basil leaves
dressing
2 teaspoons finely grated lime rind
¼ cup (60ml) lime juice
2 tablespoons coarsely chopped fresh coriander
2 fresh small red thai chillies, chopped finely
2 teaspoons peanut oil
1 teaspoon white sugar

1 Place chicken, spinach, capsicum, onion and basil in large bowl.
2 Make dressing, pour over salad; toss gently to combine.
dressing place ingredients in screw-top jar; shake well.

on the table in 20 minutes
serves 4 **per serving** 9.6g total fat (2.4g saturated fat); 924kJ (221 cal);
5.0g carbohydrate; 27.4g protein; 2.7g fibre
tip smoked chicken breast may be slightly pink, like bacon and ham, but
this does not mean it is undercooked.

stir-fries

Chicken sang choy bow

1 tablespoon peanut oil
1 fresh long red chilli, chopped finely
2 cloves garlic, crushed
400g mince
1 small red capsicum (150g), chopped finely
⅓ cup (80ml) lemon juice
½ cup (80g) blanched almonds, toasted, chopped finely
½ cup finely chopped fresh basil
2 tablespoons kecap manis
1 cup (80g) bean sprouts
100g crisp fried noodles
12 iceberg lettuce leaves

1 Heat oil in wok; stir-fry chilli and garlic until fragrant. Add chicken and capsicum; stir-fry until chicken is cooked through.
2 Add juice, nuts, basil, kecap manis and sprouts; stir-fry 1 minute. Stir in half of the noodles.
3 Divide sang choy bow among lettuce leaves; serve sprinkled with remaining noodles.

on the table in 25 minutes
serves 4 **per serving** 25.1g total fat (4.2g saturated fat); 1735kJ (415 cal); 16.2g carbohydrate; 28.3g protein; 5.0g fibre
tip crisp fried noodles are sold packaged (commonly a 100g packet) already deep-fried and ready to eat. They are sometimes labelled crunchy noodles, and are available in two widths — thin and spaghetti-like or wide and flat like fettuccine.

Honey chilli chicken

1 tablespoon peanut oil
1kg tenderloins, sliced thinly
4cm piece fresh ginger (20g), grated
3 fresh small red thai chillies, chopped finely
1 large red capsicum (350g), sliced thickly
1 teaspoon cornflour
1 tablespoon soy sauce
⅓ cup (80ml) lemon juice
¼ cup (90g) honey
4 green onions, chopped finely

1 Heat half of the oil in wok; stir-fry chicken, ginger and chilli, in batches, until chicken is browned.
2 Heat remaining oil in wok; stir-fry capsicum until just tender.
3 Blend cornflour in small jug with sauce, stir in juice and honey. Return chicken mixture to wok with honey mixture; cook, stirring, until mixture boils and thickens slightly. Sprinkle with onion just before serving.

on the table in 25 minutes
serves 4 **per serving** 10.5g total fat (2.3g saturated fat); 1756kJ (420 cal); 21.7g carbohydrate; 58.4g protein; 1.2g fibre

Warm chicken tabbouleh stir-fry

1 cup (160g) burghul
500g tenderloins, sliced thinly
2 cloves garlic, crushed
¾ cup (180ml) lemon juice
¼ cup (60ml) olive oil
250g cherry tomatoes, halved
4 green onions, chopped coarsely
1 cup chopped fresh flat-leaf parsley
1 cup chopped fresh mint

1 Place burghul in small bowl; cover with boiling water. Stand 15 minutes; drain. Using hands, squeeze out as much excess water as possible.
2 Meanwhile, combine chicken, garlic, a quarter of the juice and 1 tablespoon of the oil in medium bowl; stand 5 minutes. Drain; discard marinade.
3 Heat 1 tablespoon of the oil in wok; stir-fry chicken mixture, in batches, until chicken is browned all over and cooked through. Cover to keep warm.
4 Place burghul with tomato and onion in wok; stir-fry until onion softens. Remove from heat. Add chicken mixture, parsley, mint, remaining juice and oil; toss gently to combine.

on the table in 30 minutes
serves 4 **per serving** 17.6g total fat (2.8g saturated fat); 1772kJ (424 cal); 27.4g carbohydrate; 34.4g protein; 9.4g fibre
tip tabbouleh is a traditional Lebanese salad made with a great deal of chopped flat-leaf parsley and varying amounts of burghul, green onion, mint, olive oil and lemon juice.

Chicken and oyster sauce noodle stir-fry

375g dried rice stick noodles
2 teaspoons sesame oil
1 tablespoon peanut oil
600g thigh fillets, sliced thinly
350g asparagus, trimmed, chopped coarsely
375g fresh baby corn, halved lengthways
2 cloves garlic, crushed
¼ cup (60ml) oyster sauce
½ cup coarsely chopped fresh garlic chives

1 Place noodles in large heatproof bowl; cover with boiling water. Stand
5 minutes or until just tender; drain.
2 Meanwhile, heat half of the combined oils in wok; stir-fry chicken,
in batches, until cooked through.
3 Heat remaining combined oils in wok; stir-fry asparagus, corn and
garlic until just tender. Return chicken to wok with noodles, sauce and
chives; stir-fry until heated through.

on the table in 25 minutes
serves 4 **per serving** 20.2g total fat (4.6g saturated fat); 2780kJ
(665 cal); 80.1g carbohydrate; 39.6g protein; 6.9g fibre

Hot and sour chicken

4 cloves garlic, crushed
2 tablespoons lemon pepper seasoning
4 fresh small red thai chillies, chopped finely
½ cup (125ml) water
2 tablespoons tamarind concentrate
1kg breast fillets, sliced thinly
350g snake beans, trimmed
1 tablespoon peanut oil
2 large red onions (600g), sliced thickly
1 tablespoon white sugar
¼ cup (60ml) chicken stock

1 Combine garlic, seasoning, chilli, the water, tamarind and chicken in medium bowl; stand 10 minutes.
2 Meanwhile, boil, steam or microwave beans until just tender; drain.
3 Heat oil in wok; stir-fry chicken mixture and onion, in batches, until chicken is browned and cooked through.
4 Return chicken mixture to wok with beans, sugar and stock; stir-fry, tossing until sauce boils and thickens slightly.

on the table in 35 minutes
serves 6 **per serving** 7.2g total fat (1.6g saturated fat); 1162kJ (278 cal); 9.9g carbohydrate; 41.3g protein; 3.4g fibre

Sweet garlic chicken with choy sum

500g hokkien noodles
1 tablespoon peanut oil
750g thigh fillets, sliced thickly
8 green onions, chopped coarsely
4 cloves garlic, crushed
2cm piece fresh ginger (10g), sliced thinly
230g can sliced water chestnuts, drained
300g choy sum, trimmed, chopped coarsely
2 tablespoons coarsely chopped fresh coriander
2 tablespoons kecap manis
¼ cup (60ml) chicken stock

1 Place noodles in large heatproof bowl; cover with boiling water. Separate noodles with fork; drain.
2 Heat oil in wok; stir-fry chicken, in batches, until browned all over and cooked through.
3 Return chicken to wok with onion, garlic, ginger and water chestnuts; stir-fry until fragrant. Add choy sum, coriander, kecap manis and stock; stir-fry until choy sum just wilts. Top noodles with chicken. Serve with a dollop of sambal oelek, if desired.

on the table in 30 minutes
serves 4 **per serving** 8.5g total fat (3.3g saturated fat); 765kJ (183 cal); 15.2g carbohydrate; 10.2g protein; 2.6g fibre
tips use gai lan if choy sum is unavailable.

Chicken and almond stir-fry

2 tablespoons peanut oil
1 cup (160g) blanched whole almonds
600g tenderloins
1cm piece fresh ginger (5g), grated
2 tablespoons hoisin sauce
1 small leek (200g), sliced thickly
200g green beans, halved
2 green onions, chopped finely
1 tablespoon soy sauce
1 tablespoon plum sauce
1 teaspoon sesame oil

1 Heat half of the peanut oil in wok; stir-fry almonds until browned, remove from wok.
2 Stir-fry chicken in wok, in batches, until browned and just cooked through.
3 Heat remaining peanut oil in wok; stir-fry ginger until fragrant. Add hoisin sauce, leek and beans; stir-fry until beans are just tender.
4 Return chicken to wok with onion, soy sauce, plum sauce and sesame oil; stir-fry until heated through. Toss through almonds.

on the table in 25 minutes
serves 4 **per serving** 36.8g total fat (4.2g saturated fat); 2324kJ (556 cal); 9.1g carbohydrate; 44.4g protein; 7.1g fibre

Garlic chicken stir-fry with buk choy

700g breast fillets, sliced thinly
½ cup (75g) plain flour
2 tablespoons peanut oil
6 cloves garlic, crushed
1 medium red capsicum (200g), sliced thinly
6 green onions, sliced thinly
½ cup (125ml) chicken stock
2 tablespoons light soy sauce
500g buk choy, chopped coarsely

1 Coat chicken in flour; shake off excess.
2 Heat oil in wok; stir-fry chicken, in batches, until browned all over and cooked through.
3 Add garlic, capsicum and onion to wok; stir-fry until capsicum is tender.
4 Return chicken to wok with stock and sauce; stir-fry until sauce boils and thickens slightly. Add buk choy; stir-fry until buk choy just wilts.

on the table in 25 minutes
serves 4 **per serving** 14.0g total fat (2.8g saturated fat); 1618kJ (387 cal); 18.1g carbohydrate; 45.1g protein; 3.9g fibre

Chicken stir-fry on noodle cakes

3 x 85g packets chicken-flavoured instant noodles
2 tablespoons peanut oil
700g breast fillets, sliced thinly
1 small brown onion (80g), sliced thinly
1 clove garlic, crushed
1 medium carrot (120g), sliced thinly
1 large red capsicum (350g), sliced thinly
400g baby buk choy, quartered
2cm piece fresh ginger (10g), grated
⅓ cup (80ml) oyster sauce
2 tablespoons soy sauce
¾ cup (180ml) chicken stock
1 tablespoon cornflour

1 Cook noodles according to instructions on packet. Drain noodles, add one of the flavour sachets and stir to combine (reserve remaining sachets for another use).
2 Heat half of the oil in large frying pan, add noodles and press into a "cake" shape; cook until browned on both sides.
3 Heat remaining oil in wok; stir-fry chicken, in batches, until cooked through.
4 Add onion and garlic to wok; stir-fry until just tender. Add carrot and capsicum; stir-fry until just tender.
5 Return chicken to wok with buk choy and combined ginger, sauces, stock and cornflour; stir-fry until mixture boils and thickens.
6 Cut noodle cake into quarters. Serve stir-fry on noodle cakes.

on the table in 20 minutes
serves 4 **per serving** 16.4g total fat (2.8g saturated fat); 1814kJ (434 cal); 23.5g carbohydrate; 45.9g protein; 4.0g fibre

Chicken and mixed mushroom stir-fry

600g hokkien noodles
1 tablespoon peanut oil
750g tenderloins, halved
200g button mushrooms, halved
200g flat mushrooms, sliced thickly
200g swiss brown mushrooms, halved
3 green onions, chopped finely
2 tablespoons mild chilli sauce
½ cup (125ml) oyster sauce

1 Place noodles in large heatproof bowl; cover with boiling water.
Separate noodles with fork; drain.
2 Heat half of the oil in wok; stir-fry chicken, in batches, until browned
all over and cooked through.
3 Heat remaining oil in wok; stir-fry mushrooms, in batches, until browned.
4 Return chicken and mushrooms to wok with noodles, onion and
sauces; stir-fry until heated through.

on the table in 25 minutes
serves 4 **per serving** 11.6g total fat (2.4g saturated fat); 3064kJ
(733 cal); 8.6g carbohydrate; 63.0g protein; 8.2g fibre

Lemon grass and asparagus chicken

500g breast fillets, sliced thickly
3 cloves garlic, crushed
10cm stick (20g) fresh lemon grass, chopped finely
1 teaspoon white sugar
1cm piece fresh ginger (5g), grated finely
1 tablespoon peanut oil
400g asparagus, trimmed
1 large brown onion (200g), sliced thickly
2 medium tomatoes (300g), seeded, chopped coarsely
2 teaspoons fresh coriander
2 tablespoons roasted sesame seeds

1 Combine chicken, garlic, lemon grass, sugar, ginger and half of the oil in medium bowl.
2 Cut asparagus spears into thirds; boil, steam or microwave until just tender. Rinse immediately under cold water; drain.
3 Heat remaining oil in wok; stir-fry onion until just soft, remove from wok. Stir-fry chicken mixture, in batches, until chicken is browned and cooked through.
4 Return chicken mixture and onion to wok with asparagus and tomato; stir-fry until heated through.
5 Serve sprinkled with coriander and sesame seeds.

on the table in 30 minutes
serves 4 **per serving** 10.8g total fat (2.0g saturated fat); 1117kJ (267 cal); 7.3g carbohydrate; 33.0g protein; 4.0g fibre

Spicy chicken wings

1kg wings
1 tablespoon peanut oil
1cm piece fresh ginger (5g), grated
1 clove garlic, crushed
2 tablespoons soy sauce
¼ cup (60ml) hoisin sauce
1 tablespoon sweet chilli sauce
2 teaspoons caster sugar
½ cup (125ml) water
3 green onions, chopped finely

1 Cut wing tips from chicken; discard tips. Cut wings in half at joints.
2 Heat oil in wok; stir-fry ginger and garlic until aromatic.
3 Add sauces, sugar and the water; stir-fry 1 minute. Add chicken; cook, covered, about 15 minutes, stirring occasionally, or until chicken is cooked through. Stir in onion. Serve chicken with steamed baby buk choy, if desired.

on the table in 35 minutes
serves 4 **per serving** 13.9g total fat (3.7g saturated fat); 1325kJ (317 cal); 9.8g carbohydrate; 37.3g protein; 2.1g fibre

Chicken chow mein

1 tablespoon peanut oil
500g thigh fillets, sliced thinly
2 medium brown onions (300g), sliced thinly
2 cloves garlic, crushed
4cm piece fresh ginger (20g), grated
2 trimmed celery stalks (200g), sliced thinly
1 medium red capsicum (200g), sliced thinly
2 teaspoons cornflour
½ cup (125ml) chicken stock
¼ cup (60ml) light soy sauce
5 green onions, sliced thickly
1 cup (80g) bean sprouts
2 cups (160g) finely shredded wombok
200g crisp fried noodles

1 Heat half of the oil in wok; stir-fry chicken, in batches, until browned all over and cooked through.
2 Heat remaining oil in wok; stir-fry brown onion, garlic and ginger until fragrant. Add celery and capsicum; stir-fry until vegetables are just tender.
3 Blend cornflour with stock and sauce in small jug. Return chicken to wok with cornflour mixture; stir-fry until sauce boils and thickens slightly. Add green onion, sprouts and wombok; stir-fry until heated through.
4 Serve chow mein on crisp fried noodles.

on the table in 30 minutes
serves 4 **per serving** 15.9g total fat (4.1g saturated fat); 1768kJ (423 cal); 34.7g carbohydrate; 32.4g protein; 5.1g fibre
tips crisp fried noodles are sold packaged (commonly a 100g packet) already deep-fried and ready to eat. They are sometimes labelled crunchy noodles, and are available in two widths — thin and spaghetti-like or wide and flat like fettuccine. You will need a quarter of a large wombok for this recipe.

Chicken, pork and rice noodle stir-fry

¼ cup (55g) white sugar
⅓ cup (80ml) mild chilli sauce
¼ cup (60ml) fish sauce
1 tablespoon light soy sauce
1 tablespoon tomato sauce
500g breast fillets, sliced
150g fresh wide rice noodles
1 tablespoon sesame oil
500g pork mince
1 large brown onion (200g), sliced thickly
2 cloves garlic, crushed
2 cups (160g) bean sprouts
1 cup coarsely chopped fresh coriander
⅓ cup (50g) coarsely chopped roasted peanuts

1 Combine sugar and sauces in large bowl with chicken.
2 Place noodles in large heatproof bowl; cover with boiling water.
Separate noodles with fork; drain.
3 Drain chicken mixture; reserve marinade. Heat half of the oil in wok;
stir-fry chicken mixture, in batches, until chicken is browned all over and
cooked through.
4 Heat remaining oil in wok; stir-fry pork, onion and garlic until pork is
cooked through.
5 Return chicken to wok with noodles and reserved marinade. Stir-fry
until heated through; remove from heat. Add sprouts, coriander and
peanuts; toss gently to combine.

on the table in 25 minutes
serves 4 **per serving** 23.7g total fat (5.6g saturated fat); 2521kJ
(603 cal); 33.5g carbohydrate; 61.3g protein; 4.6g fibre
tip you can use fresh or dried rice noodles, wide or spaghetti-like –
whatever you prefer.

Chicken, coriander and cashew stir-fry

700g breast fillets, sliced thinly
¼ cup coarsely chopped fresh coriander
2 fresh small red thai chillies, chopped finely
1 teaspoon sesame oil
2 cloves garlic, crushed
2 teaspoons peanut oil
⅓ cup (80ml) rice vinegar
¼ cup (60ml) sweet chilli sauce
1 tablespoon lime juice
¼ cup (35g) raw cashews, toasted
⅔ cup (40g) snow pea sprouts
⅔ cup (40g) snow pea tendrils

1 Combine chicken, coriander, chilli, sesame oil and garlic in large bowl.
2 Heat peanut oil in wok; stir-fry chicken mixture, in batches, until browned and cooked through.
3 Return chicken mixture to wok. Add vinegar, sauce and juice; stir-fry until sauce boils. Add cashews; stir-fry until just combined.
4 Remove wok from heat; toss through sprouts and tendrils.

on the table in 35 minutes
serves 4 **per serving** 12.4g total fat (2.5g saturated fat); 1371kJ (328 cal); 9.5g carbohydrate; 43.2g protein; 2.5g fibre

Pad thai

250g dried rice stick noodles
1 tablespoon peanut oil
450g thigh fillets, sliced thinly
1 clove garlic, crushed
1cm piece fresh ginger (5g), grated
2 fresh small red thai chillies, sliced thinly
2 tablespoons grated palm sugar
2 tablespoons soy sauce
¼ cup (60ml) sweet chilli sauce
1 tablespoon fish sauce
1 tablespoon lime juice
3 green onions, sliced thinly
1 cup (80g) bean sprouts
1 cup (80g) snow pea sprouts
¼ cup coarsely chopped fresh coriander

1 Place noodles in large heatproof bowl; cover with boiling water. Stand 5 minutes or until just tender; drain.
2 Heat oil in wok; stir-fry chicken, garlic, ginger and chilli, in batches, until chicken is browned.
3 Return chicken mixture to wok with sugar, sauces and juice; stir-fry until sauce thickens slightly. Add noodles, onion and sprouts to wok; stir-fry until hot. Serve pad thai sprinkled with coriander.

on the table in 30 minutes
serves 4 **per serving** 15.5g total fat (3.4g saturated fat); 1455kJ (348 cal); 28.9g carbohydrate; 26.0g protein; 3.0g fibre

Spicy chicken with rice noodles

750g thigh fillets, chopped coarsely
2 cloves garlic, crushed
2cm piece fresh ginger (10g), grated
2 teaspoons finely chopped fresh lemon grass
1 tablespoon teriyaki sauce
1 tablespoon white sugar
1 teaspoon sambal oelek
1 teaspoon ground cumin
1 teaspoon ground coriander
500g fresh wide rice noodles
2 tablespoons sweet chilli sauce
1 tablespoon peanut oil
500g baby buk choy, quartered

1 Combine chicken, garlic, ginger, lemon grass, teriyaki sauce, sugar, sambal oelek and spices in medium bowl.
2 Place noodles in large heatproof bowl; cover with boiling water. Separate noodles with fork; drain.
3 Place noodles in medium bowl; combine with sweet chilli sauce.
4 Heat half of the oil in wok; stir-fry chicken mixture, in batches, until browned all over and cooked through.
5 Heat remaining oil in wok; stir-fry buk choy until just wilted.
6 Serve chicken mixture with buk choy and noodles.

on the table in 25 minutes
serves 4 **per serving** 18.9g total fat (5.0g saturated fat); 1977kJ (473 cal); 34.9g carbohydrate; 39.4g protein; 2.7g fibre
tip if you can't find fresh rice noodles, the chicken and buk choy can be served on a bed of steamed rice.

Chicken and gai lan stir-fry

350g fresh singapore noodles
1 tablespoon peanut oil
750g tenderloins, halved
1 large brown onion (200g), sliced thickly
3 cloves garlic, crushed
1kg gai lan, chopped coarsely
⅓ cup (80ml) oyster sauce
1 tablespoon light soy sauce

1 Place noodles in large heatproof bowl; cover with boiling water.
Separate noodles with fork; drain.
2 Heat half of the oil in wok; stir-fry chicken, in batches, until browned all over and cooked through.
3 Heat remaining oil in wok; stir-fry onion and garlic until onion softens.
4 Return chicken to wok with gai lan and sauces; stir-fry until gai lan just wilts. Toss chicken mixture with noodles to serve.

on the table in 25 minutes
serves 4 **per serving** 24.9g total fat (9.5g saturated fat); 2922kJ
(699 cal); 57.6g carbohydrate; 55.0g protein; 11.1g fibre
tip any type of fresh noodle can be used in this recipe.

Chicken tikka

2 cups (400g) jasmine rice
2 tablespoons tikka paste
2 tablespoons mango chutney
1kg thigh fillets, sliced thinly
⅓ cup (80ml) vegetable stock
½ cup (140g) yogurt
½ cup coarsely chopped fresh coriander
2 teaspoons lime juice
1 fresh small red thai chilli, sliced thinly

1 Cook rice in large saucepan of boiling water, uncovered, until just tender; drain.
2 Combine paste, chutney and chicken in large bowl.
3 Heat wok; stir-fry chicken mixture, in batches, until chicken is browned all over.
4 Add remaining ingredients to wok; bring to a boil. Reduce heat, simmer, uncovered, about 5 minutes or until chicken is cooked through. Serve chicken tikka with jasmine rice.

on the table in 25 minutes
serves 4 **per serving** 23.4g total fat (6.8g saturated fat); 3290kJ (787 cal); 86.3g carbohydrate; 55.8g protein; 2.4g fibre

Thai chicken noodle stir-fry

180g dried rice stick noodles
700g breast fillets, sliced thinly
2cm piece fresh ginger (10g), grated
2 tablespoons peanut oil
1½ cups (120g) bean sprouts
300g baby buk choy, chopped coarsely
⅓ cup (80ml) lime juice
¼ cup (60ml) sweet chilli sauce
2 teaspoons fish sauce
1½ tablespoons caster sugar
2 tablespoons chopped fresh coriander
⅓ cup torn fresh mint
4 green onions, sliced thinly

1 Place noodles in large heatproof bowl; cover with boiling water. Stand 5 minutes or until just tender; drain.
2 Combine chicken and ginger in medium bowl.
3 Heat oil in wok; stir-fry chicken mixture, in batches, until cooked through.
4 Return chicken to wok with sprouts, buk choy and combined juice, sauces, sugar, coriander and mint; stir until hot. Add onion and noodles; stir-fry until hot.

on the table in 30 minutes
serves 4 **per serving** 13.6g total fat (2.7g saturated fat); 1655kJ (396 cal); 23.1g carbohydrate; 43.4g protein; 2.9g fibre

Chicken and tamarind stir-fry

2 cups (400g) jasmine rice
700g breast fillets, sliced thinly
1 tablespoon tamarind concentrate
3 cloves garlic, crushed
2 fresh small red thai chillies, sliced thinly
2 teaspoons white sugar
1 tablespoon lime juice
1 tablespoon peanut oil
1 large brown onion (200g), sliced thickly
½ cup loosely packed fresh coriander leaves

1 Cook rice in large saucepan of boiling water, uncovered, until just tender; drain.
2 Combine chicken, tamarind, garlic, chilli, sugar and juice in medium bowl.
3 Heat half of the oil in wok; stir-fry chicken mixture, in batches, until browned all over and cooked through.
4 Heat remaining oil in wok; stir-fry onion until just softened. Return chicken to wok; toss gently to combine.
5 Serve chicken mixture with rice; sprinkle with coriander, and lemon wedges, if desired.

on the table in 25 minutes
serves 4 **per serving** 23.0g total fat (6.0g saturated fat); 3035kJ (726 cal); 84.6g carbohydrate; 43.0g protein; 2.0g fibre
tip tamarind concentrate, a thick, purple-black, ready-to-use sweet-sour paste manufactured from the pulp of tamarind tree pods, is available from most supermarkets and Asian food stores.

Chicken satay noodles

700g thigh fillets, chopped coarsely
2 teaspoons ground coriander
2 teaspoons ground cumin
2 teaspoons ground turmeric
250g hokkien noodles
6 green onions
150g fresh baby corn
2 tablespoons peanut oil
1 large carrot (180g), sliced thinly
2 tablespoons chopped fresh coriander
satay sauce
½ cup (130g) crunchy peanut butter
½ cup (125ml) coconut cream
½ cup (125ml) chicken stock
2 tablespoons sweet chilli sauce
2 tablespoons soy sauce
1 tablespoon brown sugar
1 tablespoon lime juice

1 Make satay sauce.
2 Combine chicken and spices in medium bowl.
3 Place noodles in large heatproof bowl; cover with boiling water.
Separate noodles with fork; drain.
4 Chop onions and corn diagonally into 4cm pieces.
5 Heat half of the oil in wok; stir-fry chicken, in batches, until browned.
Heat remaining oil in wok; stir-fry corn and carrot until just tender.
6 Return chicken to wok with noodles, onion, satay sauce and coriander;
stir-fry until heated through.
satay sauce whisk ingredients in medium jug until well combined.

on the table in 25 minutes
serves 4 **per serving** 56.4g total fat (19.8g saturated fat); 3933kJ
(941 cal); 52.3g carbohydrate; 51.0g protein; 12.6g fibre

Stir-fried chicken and gai lan

2 tablespoons sesame oil
500g thigh fillets, sliced thinly
2 teaspoons sambal oelek
190g can sliced water chestnuts, drained
227g can bamboo shoot strips, drained
1 large red capsicum (350g), sliced thinly
⅓ cup (80ml) kecap manis
500g gai lan, chopped coarsely
2 cups (160g) bean sprouts

1 Heat half of the oil in wok; stir-fry chicken, in batches, until browned lightly all over.
2 Heat remaining oil in wok; stir-fry sambal oelek, water chestnuts, bamboo shoots and capsicum.
3 Return chicken to wok with kecap manis and gai lan; stir-fry until gai lan is just wilted and chicken is cooked through. Remove from heat; stir in sprouts.

on the table in 25 minutes
serves 4 **per serving** 18.9g total fat (4.0g saturated fat); 1384kJ (331 cal); 9.3g carbohydrate; 28.5g protein; 5.2g fibre

Spicy noodle, vegetable and chicken stir-fry

200g dried egg noodles
2 tablespoons vegetable oil
600g breast fillets, sliced thinly
1 large carrot (180g), sliced thinly
250g button mushrooms, sliced thickly
2cm piece fresh ginger (10g), grated
¼ cup (60ml) chicken stock
¼ cup (60ml) oyster sauce
2 tablespoons soy sauce
4 green onions, sliced thinly
2 long red chillies, sliced thinly
150g sugar snap peas

1 Cook noodles in large saucepan of boiling water, uncovered, until just tender; drain. Rinse under cold water; drain.
2 Meanwhile, heat half of the oil in wok; stir-fry chicken, in batches, until just cooked through.
3 Heat remaining oil in wok; stir-fry carrot, mushroom and ginger until vegetables are just tender.
4 Return chicken to wok with combined stock and sauces; stir-fry until hot. Add noodles, onion, chilli and peas; stir-fry until heated through.

on the table in 25 minutes
serves 4 **per serving** 14.0g total fat (2.3g saturated fat); 2073kJ (496 cal); 44.0g carbohydrate; 45.4g protein; 5.2g fibre

Chicken and thai basil fried rice

¼ cup (60ml) peanut oil
1 medium brown onion (150g), chopped finely
3 cloves garlic, crushed
2 long green chillies, chopped finely
1 tablespoon brown sugar
500g breast fillets, chopped coarsely
2 medium red capsicums (400g), sliced thinly
200g green beans, chopped coarsely
4 cups cooked jasmine rice
2 tablespoons fish sauce
2 tablespoons soy sauce
½ cup loosely packed thai basil leaves

1 Heat oil in wok; stir-fry onion, garlic and chilli until onion softens. Add sugar; stir-fry until dissolved. Add chicken; stir-fry until lightly browned. Add capsicum and beans; stir-fry until vegetables are just tender and chicken is cooked through.
2 Add rice and sauces; stir-fry, tossing gently to combine. Remove from heat; add basil, toss gently to combine.

on the table in 30 minutes
serves 4 **per serving** 18.0g total fat (3.4g saturated fat); 4427kJ (1059 cal); 172.8g carbohydrate; 46.4g protein; 5.1g fibre
tip you will need to cook about 1⅓ cups (265g) rice for this recipe.

Chicken and broccoli with oyster sauce

½ cup (125ml) chicken stock
¼ cup (60ml) oyster sauce
2 teaspoons cornflour
2 teaspoons caster sugar
½ teaspoon sesame oil
1 tablespoon vegetable oil
500g breast fillets, sliced thinly
4 green onions, chopped
4cm piece fresh ginger (20g), grated
1 clove garlic, crushed
500g broccoli florets
2 tablespoons water

1 Whisk stock, sauce, cornflour, sugar and sesame oil in small bowl until well combined.
2 Heat half of the vegetable oil in wok; stir-fry chicken, in batches, until just cooked through.
3 Heat remaining vegetable oil in wok; stir-fry onion, ginger, garlic, broccoli and the water until broccoli is tender.
4 Return chicken to wok with sauce mixture; stir-fry until chicken is hot and sauce boils and thickens slightly.

on the table in 20 minutes
serves 4 **per serving** 8.8g total fat (1.5g saturated fat); 1124kJ (269 cal); 9.2g carbohydrate; 35.2g protein; 5.6g fibre

Wok-tossed honey soy wings

12 large wings (1.5kg)
3 cloves garlic, crushed
4cm piece fresh ginger (40g), grated
1 tablespoon peanut oil
1 tablespoon fish sauce
1 tablespoon light soy sauce
¼ cup (90g) honey
2 green onions, sliced thinly

1 Cut wing tips from chicken; cut wings in half at joint.
2 Combine chicken in large bowl with garlic and ginger.
3 Heat oil in wok; stir-fry chicken mixture, in batches, until chicken is lightly browned.
4 Return chicken mixture to wok. Add sauces and honey; stir-fry until well coated. Cover wok; cook, stirring occasionally, about 10 minutes or until chicken is cooked through. Top with onion.

on the table in 25 minutes
serves 4 **per serving** 17.2g total fat (4.9g saturated fat); 1914kJ (458 cal); 19.9g carbohydrate; 55.1g protein; 0.8g fibre

Chicken satay

1 tablespoon peanut oil
800g tenderloins, halved
2 large brown onions (400g), sliced thickly
1 clove garlic, crushed
¼ cup (60ml) chicken stock
⅔ cup (160ml) coconut milk
¾ cup (180ml) satay sauce

1 Heat oil in wok; stir-fry chicken, in batches, until browned all over and cooked through.
2 Place onion and garlic in wok; stir-fry until onion softens. Return chicken to wok with remaining ingredients; stir-fry until sauce thickens slightly. Serve topped with green onion curls, if desired.

on the table in 20 minutes
serves 4 **per serving** 40.6g total fat (14.3g saturated fat); 2621kJ (627 cal); 19.7g carbohydrate; 45.2g protein; 2.6g fibre
tip the spiciness of this dish will depend on which brand of satay sauce you use.

Chicken, vegetable and rice noodle stir-fry

500g fresh wide rice noodles
1 tablespoon sesame oil
500g breast fillets, sliced thinly
250g oyster mushrooms, sliced thinly
¼ cup (60ml) oyster sauce
1 tablespoon fish sauce
1 tablespoon white sugar
2 teaspoons sambal oelek
250g baby spinach leaves
¼ cup coarsely chopped fresh coriander

1 Place noodles in large heatproof bowl; cover with boiling water.
Separate noodles with fork; drain.
2 Heat oil in wok; stir-fry chicken, in batches, until browned all over
and cooked through.
3 Add mushrooms to wok; stir-fry until just tender. Return chicken
to wok with noodles, sauces, sugar and sambal oelek; stir-fry until
heated through.
4 Remove from heat. Add baby spinach and coriander; toss gently
to combine.

on the table in 20 minutes
serves 4 **per serving** 8.3g total fat (1.4g saturated fat); 1538kJ (368 cal);
34.6g carbohydrate; 35.4g protein; 5.3g fibre

Chicken, chilli and kaffir lime stir-fry

2 tablespoons vegetable oil
500g breast fillets, sliced thinly
2 medium zucchini (240g), sliced thinly
4cm piece fresh ginger (20g), grated
6 green onions, sliced thickly
½ cup (125ml) water
2 tablespoons lime juice
¼ cup (60ml) oyster sauce
¼ cup (60ml) sweet chilli sauce
5 kaffir lime leaves, shredded
1 cup loosely packed thai basil leaves
3 cups (240g) bean sprouts

1 Heat half of the oil in wok; stir-fry chicken, in batches, until browned lightly all over.
2 Heat remaining oil in wok; stir-fry zucchini, ginger and onion until zucchini is just tender.
3 Return chicken to wok with combined water, juice, sauces and lime leaves; stir-fry until chicken is cooked through. Add basil and bean sprouts; stir-fry until combined.

on the table in 25 minutes
serves 4 **per serving** 12.8g total fat (2.0g saturated fat); 1200kJ (287 cal); 8.6g carbohydrate; 32.1g protein; 4.2g fibre

Curried chicken and coconut stir-fry

2 tablespoons peanut oil
700g thigh fillets, sliced thinly
1 large brown onion (200g), sliced thinly
2 cloves garlic, crushed
¼ cup (60g) madras curry paste
3 medium egg tomatoes (225g), chopped coarsely
1 cup (250ml) coconut cream
½ cup (125ml) chicken stock
2 tablespoons chopped fresh coriander
1 teaspoon brown sugar
2 tablespoons lemon juice

1 Heat half of the oil in wok; stir-fry chicken, in batches, until cooked through.
2 Heat remaining oil in wok; stir-fry onion and garlic until onion is just tender. Add curry paste; stir-fry until fragrant.
3 Return chicken to wok with tomato, coconut cream, stock, coriander, sugar and juice; stir-fry until heated through. Serve with naan bread and basmati rice, if desired.

on the table in 25 minutes
serves 4 **per serving** 39.6g total fat (17.4g saturated fat); 2257kJ (540 cal); 8.8g carbohydrate; 36.4g protein; 4.3g fibre

Chicken tuscany

700g breast fillets, sliced thinly
½ teaspoon sweet paprika
¼ cup (60ml) olive oil
2 medium brown onions (300g), sliced
3 cloves garlic, crushed
2 medium tomatoes (300g), seeded, sliced
1 tablespoon drained capers
2 tablespoons tomato paste
¼ cup (60ml) dry white wine
¼ cup (60ml) chicken stock
500g frozen broad beans, cooked, peeled
¼ cup firmly packed fresh basil leaves
⅓ cup (90g) black olive paste
¼ cup (20g) flaked parmesan cheese

1 Combine chicken and paprika in large bowl.
2 Heat 1 tablespoon of the oil in wok; stir-fry chicken mixture, onion and garlic, in batches, until chicken is browned and cooked through.
3 Heat remaining oil in wok; stir-fry tomato and capers until tender.
4 Return chicken mixture to wok with combined paste, wine and stock; stir-fry until sauce boils.
5 Add broad beans and basil to wok; stir-fry, tossing, until hot.
6 Serve chicken mixture topped with olive paste and cheese.

on the table in 25 minutes
serves 4 **per serving** 20.1g total fat (4.1g saturated fat); 2161kJ (517 cal); 22.1g carbohydrate; 51.1g protein; 14.1g fibre

Almond chicken and noodles

700g breast fillets, sliced thickly
2 cloves garlic, crushed
¼ cup (60ml) hoisin sauce
¼ cup (60ml) kecap manis
2 tablespoons peanut oil
½ cup (80g) blanched almonds
4 green onions, sliced thinly
1 medium brown onion (150g), sliced thinly
420g fresh egg noodles
200g choy sum, chopped coarsely
1 cup (250ml) chicken stock

1 Combine chicken, garlic, 2 tablespoons of the hoisin sauce and
1 tablespoon of the kecap manis in medium bowl.
2 Heat 2 teaspoons of the oil in wok; stir-fry almonds until browned.
Remove from wok.
3 Heat remaining oil in wok; stir-fry chicken mixture and onions, in
batches, until chicken is browned.
4 Place noodles in large heatproof bowl, cover with boiling water,
stand 5 minutes or until just tender; drain.
5 Return chicken mixture to wok with almonds, noodles, choy sum,
stock and remaining hoisin sauce and kecap manis; stir-fry until
choy sum is just wilted.

on the table in 20 minutes
serves 4 **per serving** 26.7g total fat (3.8g saturated fat); 3114kJ
(745 cal); 65.1g carbohydrate; 56.7g protein; 7.1g fibre

Chicken chermoulla

700g thigh fillets, sliced thinly
½ cup coarsely chopped fresh flat-leaf parsley
1 tablespoon finely grated lemon rind
1 tablespoon lemon juice
2 teaspoons ground turmeric
½ teaspoon cayenne pepper
1 tablespoon ground coriander
1 medium red onion (170g), chopped finely
2 tablespoons olive oil
1 cup (200g) red lentils
2½ cups (625ml) chicken stock
200g baby spinach leaves
½ cup coarsely chopped fresh coriander
½ cup coarsely chopped fresh mint
1 tablespoon red wine vinegar
⅓ cup (95g) yogurt

1 Combine chicken, parsley, rind, juice, spices, onion and half of the oil in large bowl.
2 Heat wok; stir-fry chicken mixture, in batches, until chicken is browned and cooked through.
3 Combine lentils and stock in medium saucepan; bring to a boil. Reduce heat, simmer, uncovered, about 8 minutes or until just tender; drain.
4 Place lentils in large bowl with spinach, coriander, mint and combined vinegar and remaining oil; toss gently to combine.
5 Serve chicken mixture on lentil mixture; drizzle with yogurt and, if desired, small mint leaves.

on the table in 30 minutes
serves 4 **per serving** 24.4g total fat (6.1g saturated fat); 2236kJ (535 cal); 24.5g carbohydrate; 49.9g protein; 9.8g fibre
tip chermoulla is a Moroccan blend of herbs and spices traditionally used for preserving or seasoning meat and fish. We used our chermoulla blend here as a quick baste for chicken, but you can also make it for use as a sauce or marinade.

Chicken and snake beans with holy basil

700g snake beans
1 tablespoon peanut oil
700g thigh fillets, chopped coarsely
2 medium white onions (300g), sliced thickly
3 cloves garlic, crushed
1 teaspoon five-spice powder
½ cup (125ml) oyster sauce
2 tablespoons light soy sauce
½ cup (75g) cashews, toasted
½ cup loosely packed fresh holy basil leaves

1 Cut snake beans into 5cm lengths.
2 Heat half of the oil in wok; stir-fry chicken, in batches, until browned all over and cooked through.
3 Heat remaining oil in wok; stir-fry onion, garlic and five-spice until onion softens. Add beans; stir-fry until beans are tender.
4 Return chicken to wok with sauces and nuts; stir-fry until sauce boils and thickens slightly. Just before serving, stir in basil.

on the table in 20 minutes
serves 4 **per serving** 27.4g total fat (6.3g saturated fat); 2098kJ (502 cal); 17.0g carbohydrate; 44.0g protein; 7.0g fibre
tips in this dish we've used holy basil, also known as kra pao or hot basil. If you can't find it, use ordinary sweet basil instead. Snake beans are long, thin green beans that are Asian in origin; use green beans if unavailable.

Sweet soy chicken and noodles

250g soba noodles
1 tablespoon peanut oil
600g breast fillets, sliced
200g sugar snap peas
2 tablespoons kecap manis
4 green onions, sliced thinly
6 red radishes (90g), sliced thinly
2 tablespoons finely chopped fresh coriander leaves

1 Cook noodles in large saucepan of boiling water, uncovered, until just tender; drain. Rinse under cold water; drain.
2 Heat half the oil in wok; stir-fry chicken, in batches, until tender.
3 Heat remaining oil in wok; stir-fry peas until just tender. Return chicken to wok with kecap manis, onion and radish; cook, stirring, until hot.
4 Combine noodles and coriander in large bowl; serve topped with chicken mixture.

on the table in 25 minutes
serves 4 **per serving** 19.1g total fat (7.1g saturated fat); 2119kJ (507 cal); 36.6g carbohydrate; 42.3g protein; 6.8g fibre

Combination stir-fry

250g uncooked medium prawns
2 tablespoons peanut oil
250g breast fillets, chopped finely
2 medium brown onions (300g), sliced thinly
2cm piece fresh ginger (10g), grated finely
2 cloves garlic, crushed
250g pork mince
3 trimmed celery stalks (300g), sliced thinly
1 large carrot (180g), sliced thinly
225g can bamboo shoots, drained, sliced thinly
½ small wombok (350g), shredded finely
⅓ cup oyster sauce (80ml)
2 tablespoons soy sauce

1 Shell and devein prawns, leaving tails intact.
2 Heat half the oil in wok; stir-fry chicken, onion, ginger and garlic, in batches, until chicken is cooked through.
3 Heat 1 teaspoon of the remaining oil in wok; stir-fry prawns until changed in colour. Remove from wok.
4 Heat 1 teaspoon of the remaining oil in wok; stir-fry pork until browned and cooked through. Remove from wok.
5 Heat remaining oil in wok; stir-fry celery and carrot until just tender. Return chicken mixture, prawns and pork to wok with bamboo shoots, wombok and sauces; stir-fry until combined and heated through.

on the table in 35 minutes
serves 4 **per serving** 15.6g total fat (3.8g saturated fat); 1440kJ (344 cal); 12.0g carbohydrate; 36.6g protein; 4.8g fibre

Chicken larb

2 tablespoons white long-grain rice
1 tablespoon peanut oil
10cm stick (20g) fresh lemon grass, chopped finely
2 fresh small red thai chillies, chopped finely
2 cloves garlic, crushed
1 tablespoon finely chopped fresh galangal
750g mince
1 lebanese cucumber (130g), seeded, sliced thinly
1 small red onion (100g), sliced thinly
1¼ cups (100g) bean sprouts
½ cup loosely packed fresh thai basil leaves
1 cup loosely packed fresh coriander leaves
4 large iceberg lettuce leaves
dressing
⅓ cup (80ml) lime juice
2 tablespoons fish sauce
2 tablespoons kecap manis
2 tablespoons peanut oil
2 teaspoons grated palm sugar

1 Make dressing.
2 Heat dry wok; stir-fry rice until browned lightly. Blend or process rice (or crush using mortar and pestle) until it resembles fine breadcrumbs.
3 Heat oil in wok; stir-fry lemon grass, chilli, garlic and galangal until fragrant. Remove from wok.
4 Stir-fry chicken, in batches, until cooked through.
5 Return chicken and lemon grass mixture to wok with about one-third of the dressing; stir-fry about 5 minutes or until mixture thickens slightly.
6 Place remaining dressing in large bowl with chicken mixture, cucumber, onion, sprouts and herbs; toss gently to combine. Place lettuce leaves on serving plates; divide larb salad among leaves, sprinkle with ground rice.
dressing place ingredients in screw-top jar; shake well.

on the table in 35 minutes
serves 4 **per serving** 29.1g total fat (7.0g saturated fat); 1969kJ (471 cal); 11.9g carbohydrate; 40.0g protein; 0.8g fibre

Honey soy chicken

¼ cup (90g) honey
¼ cup (60ml) soy sauce
½ teaspoon five-spice powder
1 tablespoon dry sherry
1 clove garlic, crushed
1cm piece fresh ginger (5g), grated
700g breast fillets, sliced thinly
1 tablespoon peanut oil
1 large brown onion (200g), sliced thinly
1 tablespoon sesame seeds
500g baby buk choy, quartered
500g choy sum, chopped coarsely

1 Place honey, sauce, five-spice, sherry, garlic and ginger in screw-top jar; shake well. Place chicken in medium bowl, combine with half the honey mixture; stand 10 minutes.
2 Drain chicken; discard marinade. Heat half of the oil in wok; stir-fry chicken and onion, in batches, until chicken is browned.
3 Heat remaining oil in wok; stir-fry seeds until lightly browned. Return chicken to wok with buk choy, choy sum and remaining honey mixture; stir-fry until vegetables are just wilted.

on the table in 35 minutes
serves 4 **per serving** 10.7g total fat (2.1g saturated fat); 1588kJ (380 cal); 22.5g carbohydrate; 44.6g protein; 4.3g fibre
tip add 1 finely chopped red chilli to the marinade, if desired.

Teriyaki chicken and cashew stir-fry with noodles

450g hokkien noodles
2 tablespoons peanut oil
1kg thigh fillets, sliced thinly
1 medium brown onion (150g), sliced thinly
1 clove garlic, crushed
2cm piece fresh ginger (10g), grated
1 medium red capsicum (200g), sliced thinly
1 tablespoon brown sugar
2 tablespoons soy sauce
½ cup (125ml) teriyaki sauce
500g choy sum, chopped coarsely
½ cup (75g) unsalted roasted cashews

1 Place noodles in large heatproof bowl; cover with boiling water. Separate noodles with fork; drain.
2 Heat half of the oil in wok; stir-fry chicken, in batches, until browned lightly.
3 Heat remaining oil in wok; stir-fry onion, garlic, ginger and capsicum about 3 minutes or until onion is just tender.
4 Return chicken to wok with sugar, sauces and choy sum; stir-fry until chicken is cooked through and choy sum wilted. Add noodles and half of the nuts; toss gently until heated through. Serve stir-fry topped with remaining nuts.

on the table in 35 minutes
serves 6 **per serving** 24.9g total fat (6.0g saturated fat); 2103kJ (503 cal); 27.6g carbohydrate; 40.4g protein; 4.0g fibre

Chilli-chicken stir-fry with asian greens

2½ cups (500g) jasmine rice
1 tablespoon sesame oil
4 breast fillets (800g), sliced thinly
2 cloves garlic, crushed
1 large red capsicum (350g), sliced thinly
⅓ cup (100g) thai chilli jam
2 tablespoons sweet chilli sauce
¼ cup (60ml) chicken stock
500g baby buk choy, halved lengthways
225g can water chestnuts, drained, halved
4 green onions, sliced thinly
1 tablespoon sesame seeds, toasted

1 Cook rice in large saucepan of boiling water, uncovered, until just tender; drain. Cover to keep warm.
2 Meanwhile, heat half of the oil in wok; stir-fry chicken, in batches, until cooked through. Return chicken to wok with garlic, capsicum, jam, sauce and stock; stir-fry until sauce thickens slightly. Remove from wok.
3 Heat remaining oil in cleaned wok; stir-fry buk choy, chestnuts and onion until buk choy just wilts. Add chicken mixture; stir until combined.
4 Sprinkle with sesame seeds. Serve with rice.

on the table in 25 minutes
serves 4 **per serving** 13.7g total fat (2.7g saturated fat); 3490kJ (835 cal); 115.9g carbohydrate; 57.6g protein; 5.4g fibre

Cajun chicken with tomato salsa

750g breast fillets, sliced thinly
¼ cup cajun seasoning
2 teaspoons grated lime rind
2 trimmed corn cobs (500g)
2 tablespoons olive oil
1 small red onion (100g), cut into thin wedges
tomato salsa
2 small egg tomatoes (120g), chopped finely
2 green onions, sliced thinly
2 teaspoons lime juice
2 teaspoons balsamic vinegar

1 Make tomato salsa.
2 Combine chicken, seasoning and rind in large bowl. Cut corn kernels from cobs.
3 Heat half of the oil in wok; stir-fry chicken mixture, in batches, until cooked through.
4 Heat remaining oil in wok; stir-fry corn and onion until onion is soft. Return chicken to wok; stir-fry until hot.
5 Serve chicken mixture topped with tomato salsa.
tomato salsa combine ingredients in small bowl.

on the table in 35 minutes
serves 4 **per serving** 14.6g total fat (2.5g saturated fat); 1668kJ (399 cal); 17.3g carbohydrate; 47.0g protein; 5.0g fibre

Chicken and corn with egg rolls

2 eggs
1 tablespoon peanut oil
130g can creamed corn
4cm piece fresh ginger (20g), chopped finely
1 clove garlic, crushed
1 fresh small red thai chilli, chopped finely
1 small white onion (80g), chopped
½ cup (125ml) chicken stock
700g thigh fillets
100g fresh baby corn
1 medium red capsicum (200g), sliced
6 green onions, sliced

1 Whisk eggs and 1 teaspoon of the oil in small jug.
2 Brush heated wok with a little of the remaining oil. Add half of the egg mixture, swirling wok to form a thin omelette; remove from wok. Repeat with remaining egg mixture. Roll omelettes tightly; cut into thin slices.
3 Blend or process creamed corn, ginger, garlic, chilli, white onion and stock until almost smooth.
4 Cut each chicken fillet into thirds.
5 Heat remaining oil in wok; stir-fry chicken, in batches, until browned and cooked through.
6 Stir-fry baby corn and capsicum in wok until just tender. Return chicken to wok with creamed corn mixture; stir-fry until sauce boils.
7 Add green onion and egg roll slices; stir-fry to combine.

on the table in 35 minutes
serves 4 **per serving** 20.6g total fat (5.6g saturated fat); 1685kJ (403 cal); 13.7g carbohydrate; 39.3g protein; 3.6g fibre

Fried noodles, chicken and buk choy

250g dried rice stick noodles
1 tablespoon peanut oil
3 eggs, beaten lightly
1 medium brown onion (150g), chopped finely
2 cloves garlic, crushed
2cm piece fresh ginger (10g), grated
500g mince
500g baby buk choy, chopped coarsely
¼ cup (60ml) soy sauce
½ cup chopped fresh coriander
3 cups (240g) bean sprouts

1 Place noodles in large heatproof bowl; cover with boiling water. Stand 5 minutes or until just tender; drain.
2 Brush heated wok with a little of the oil. Add half of the egg, swirl to cover base of wok; cook until set. Remove omelette from wok; repeat with remaining egg. Roll omelettes tightly; slice thinly.
3 Heat remaining oil in wok; stir-fry onion, garlic and ginger until onion softens. Add chicken; stir-fry until chicken is cooked through. Add buk choy, sauce and coriander; stir-fry until buk choy is just tender. Stir in noodles and sprouts. Serve topped with omelette.

on the table in 30 minutes
serves 4 **per serving** 19.1g total fat (5.0g saturated fat); 1601kJ (383 cal); 15.7g carbohydrate; 34.7g protein; 4.7g fibre

Chicken and oyster sauce stir-fry

1 tablespoon sesame oil
1 tablespoon peanut oil
750g thigh fillets, sliced thickly
175g broccolini, chopped coarsely
230g fresh baby corn, halved lengthways
2 cloves garlic, crushed
½ cup (125ml) oyster sauce
1 tablespoon rice wine vinegar
2 tablespoons water
½ cup coarsely chopped fresh garlic chives

1 Heat half of the combined oils in wok; stir-fry chicken, in batches, until cooked through.
2 Heat remaining oils in wok; stir-fry broccolini, corn and garlic until vegetables are just tender.
3 Return chicken to wok with combined sauce, vinegar and water until heated through. Stir in chives.

on the table in 25 minutes
serves 4 **per serving** 23.9g total fat (5.6g saturated fat); 1914kJ (458 cal); 18.2g carbohydrate; 40.6g protein; 4.8g fibre

Chengdu chicken

800g breast fillets, chopped coarsely
2 tablespoons light soy sauce
2 tablespoons chinese cooking wine
1 teaspoon sesame oil
¼ cup (60ml) peanut oil
300g spinach, trimmed, chopped coarsely
2 cloves garlic, crushed
2cm piece fresh ginger (10g), grated
4 green onions, sliced thinly
1 tablespoon rice vinegar
1 teaspoon white sugar
2 tablespoons finely grated orange rind
2 tablespoons sambal oelek
1 teaspoon sichuan peppercorns, crushed

1 Combine chicken, half the sauce, half the wine and half the sesame oil in large bowl.
2 Heat 1 tablespoon of the peanut oil in wok; stir-fry spinach until just wilted. Remove from wok; cover to keep warm.
3 Heat half the remaining peanut oil in wok; stir-fry chicken mixture, in batches, until browned. Heat remaining peanut oil in wok; stir-fry garlic, ginger and onion until onion just softens.
4 Return chicken and remaining sauce, wine and sesame oil to wok with vinegar, sugar, rind and sambal; stir-fry until chicken is cooked.
5 Serve spinach topped with chicken; sprinkle with pepper.

on the table in 35 minutes
serves 4 **per serving** 19.8g total fat (3.8g saturated fat); 1710kJ (409 cal); 5.7g carbohydrate; 48.0g protein; 2.1g fibre

pan-fries

Farfalle with tenderloins, ricotta, spinach and tomato

375g farfalle pasta
1 tablespoon olive oil
1 medium brown onion (150g), chopped finely
1 clove garlic, crushed
600g tenderloins, chopped coarsely
150g baby spinach leaves
1 cup (200g) ricotta cheese
1 egg
2 teaspoons finely grated lemon rind
2 tablespoons lemon juice
200g grape tomatoes, halved
¼ cup (20g) finely grated parmesan cheese

1 Cook pasta in large saucepan of boiling water, uncovered, until just tender; drain.
2 Meanwhile, heat oil in large deep frying pan; cook onion and garlic, stirring, until onion softens. Add chicken; cook, stirring, over medium heat, about 5 minutes or until cooked through.
3 Place chicken mixture and drained pasta in large serving bowl with spinach, combined ricotta and egg, rind, juice and tomato; toss gently to combine.
4 Serve sprinkled with parmesan and cracked black pepper.

on the table in 25 minutes
serves 4 **per serving** 20.7g total fat (7.7g saturated fat); 2851kJ (682 cal); 67.7g carbohydrate; 52.2g protein; 5.6g fibre

Lemon and anchovy chicken with garlic pumpkin

800g piece butternut pumpkin, peeled
2 tablespoons olive oil
4 cloves garlic, sliced thinly
½ cup (125ml) chicken stock
12 fresh sage leaves
4 breast fillets (800g)
40g butter
3 anchovy fillets, drained, chopped finely
1 tablespoon lemon juice

1 Chop pumpkin into 1.5cm pieces. Heat half of the oil in large saucepan; cook pumpkin and garlic, stirring, until it begins to brown. Add 2 tablespoons of the stock; cover and steam for 5 minutes or until pumpkin is just tender. Stir in sage.
2 Meanwhile, cut chicken in half horizontally to give eight thin pieces. Melt half of the butter and remaining oil in large frying pan; add chicken and cook until browned on both sides and just cooked through. Remove chicken from pan; keep warm.
3 Add remaining butter to same pan with anchovy; cook, stirring, until butter melts. Add juice and remaining stock; simmer, uncovered, 1 minute or until reduced slightly.
4 Serve pumpkin topped with chicken and sauce. Serve with rocket or a green salad, if desired.

on the table in 25 minutes
serves 4 **per serving** 23.4g total fat (8.6g saturated fat); 1969kJ (471 cal); 11.2g carbohydrate; 52.7g protein; 2.5g fibre

Chicken, chorizo and capsicum pasta

375g caserecci pasta (or other short pasta)
⅓ cup (80ml) extra virgin olive oil
1 chilli chorizo (300g), sliced thinly
1 medium red capsicum (200g), sliced thinly
400g breast fillets, sliced thinly
2 cloves garlic, crushed
½ cup (60g) green olives
½ cup coarsely chopped fresh flat-leaf parsley

1 Cook pasta in large saucepan of boiling water, uncovered, until just tender; drain.
2 Meanwhile, heat 1 tablespoon of the oil in large frying pan; cook chorizo and capsicum, stirring, until the capsicum softens. Remove from pan.
3 Add chicken to same pan; cook, stirring, until browned and just cooked through.
4 Add garlic and olives to chicken mixture; cook, stirring, 2 minutes. Toss chicken mixture with remaining oil, parsley and pasta.

on the table in 30 minutes
serves 4 **per serving** 47.5g total fat (12.7g saturated fat); 3804kJ (910 cal); 71.1g carbohydrate; 47.5g protein; 4.7g fibre

Sumac-flavoured drumettes with tomato, rocket and herb salad

20 drumettes (1.4kg)
¼ cup (25g) sumac
¼ cup (60ml) olive oil
1 lebanese cucumber (130g), halved lengthways, sliced thickly
2 medium tomatoes (300g), chopped coarsely
1 medium green capsicum (200g), chopped finely
¾ cup coarsely chopped fresh flat-leaf parsley
¼ cup coarsely chopped fresh mint
50g baby rocket leaves
2 tablespoons lemon juice

1 Combine chicken and sumac in large bowl.
2 Heat 2 tablespoons of the oil in large frying pan; cook chicken, in batches, covered, turning occasionally until browned and cooked through.
3 Place remaining oil in large bowl with cucumber, tomato, capsicum, herbs, rocket and juice; toss gently to combine.
4 Serve chicken with salad.

on the table in 30 minutes
serves 4 **per serving** 34.9g total fat (8.3g saturated fat); 1986kJ (475 cal); 3.8g carbohydrate; 35.6g protein; 2.4g fibre

Chicken with pistachio sauce and kumara mash

2 medium kumara (800g), chopped coarsely
⅓ cup (80ml) hot milk
20g butter
4 breast fillets (800g)
2 teaspoons olive oil
½ cup (125ml) dry white wine
½ cup (125ml) chicken stock
⅔ cup (160ml) cream
2 tablespoons hot water
2 teaspoons fresh lemon thyme leaves
¼ cup (35g) toasted shelled pistachios, chopped coarsely
350g green beans

1 Boil, steam or microwave kumara until tender; drain. Mash kumara with milk and half of the butter in medium bowl.
2 Slice chicken in half horizontally. Heat oil and remaining butter in large frying pan; cook chicken, in batches, until cooked through. Cover to keep warm.
3 Place wine in same pan; bring to a boil. Stir in stock and cream; reduce heat, simmer, uncovered, about 10 minutes or until sauce thickens slightly. Stir in the hot water, thyme and nuts.
4 Meanwhile, boil, steam or microwave beans until tender; drain.
5 Serve chicken and sauce with kumara mash and beans.

on the table in 35 minutes
serves 4 **per serving** 30.7g total fat (14.8g saturated fat); 2525kJ (604 cal); 30.0g carbohydrate; 47.3g protein; 6.2g fibre

Thai lime chicken with buk choy

1 tablespoon peanut oil
8 thigh fillets (880g)
300g baby buk choy, quartered lengthways
1 lime, cut into four slices
2 green onions, sliced thinly
¼ cup firmly packed fresh coriander leaves
dressing
1 tablespoon fish sauce
2 tablespoons lime juice
2 tablespoons grated palm sugar
1 clove garlic, crushed
1 fresh small red thai chilli, chopped finely

1 Heat oil in large frying pan; cook chicken, in batches, until cooked through.
2 Make dressing.
3 Boil, steam or microwave buk choy until tender; drain.
4 Add lime slices to same frying pan; cook until browned both sides.
5 Divide chicken among serving plates; spoon dressing over chicken, top with onion and coriander. Serve with buk choy, lime slices and steamed jasmine rice, if desired.
dressing place ingredients in screw-top jar; shake well.

on the table in 25 minutes
serves 4 **per serving** 20.7g total fat (5.7g saturated fat); 1622kJ (388 cal); 7.9g carbohydrate; 42.5g protein; 1.8g fibre

Creamy chicken with tarragon and crisp potatoes

vegetable oil, for shallow-frying
500g frozen crunchy potato cubes
8 thigh fillets (880g)
¼ cup (35g) plain flour
1 tablespoon olive oil
2 tablespoons fresh tarragon leaves
¼ cup (60ml) dry white wine
½ cup (125ml) chicken stock
¼ cup (60ml) thickened cream
200g green beans

1 Heat vegetable oil in large frying pan; shallow-fry potato, in batches, until crisp and hot. Remove from pan with a slotted spoon; drain on absorbent paper.
2 Toss chicken in flour, shake away excess flour. Heat olive oil in large frying pan over high heat, add chicken, smooth-side down, and cook until browned underneath. Turn chicken, sprinkle with tarragon, cover pan and cook until just cooked through. Remove from pan.
3 Add wine and stock to same pan, bring to a boil; boil, stirring, until reduced by half. Add cream; stir until well-combined and hot.
4 Boil, steam or microwave beans until just tender; drain well.
5 Serve chicken and sauce with potatoes and beans.

on the table in 35 minutes
serves 4 **per serving** 46.5g total fat (15.7g saturated fat); 3741kJ (895 cal); 64.0g carbohydrate; 49.7g protein; 7.4g fibre

Chicken with mustard and sun-dried tomato sauce

30g butter
1 clove garlic, crushed
4 breast fillets (800g)
¾ cup (180ml) chicken stock
1 tablespoon wholegrain mustard
¼ cup (35g) drained sun-dried tomatoes, chopped finely
4 green onions, chopped finely

1 Heat butter in large frying pan; cook garlic, stirring, 1 minute. Add chicken; cook until browned and cooked through. Remove from pan.
2 Add stock to same pan; bring to a boil, stirring. Reduce heat, simmer, uncovered, 5 minutes. Stir in mustard, tomato and onion.
3 Serve sliced chicken drizzled with sauce; accompany with roasted potato slices, if desired.

on the table in 25 minutes
serves 4 **per serving** 11.8g total fat (5.4g saturated fat); 1321kJ (316 cal); 4.2g carbohydrate; 47.2g protein; 1.8g fibre

Lemon chicken

4 breast fillets (800g)
2 egg whites, beaten lightly
½ cup (75g) plain flour
30g butter
2 tablespoons vegetable oil
1½ tablespoons cornflour
1 tablespoon brown sugar
½ cup (125ml) lemon juice
1cm piece fresh ginger (5g), grated
1 teaspoon soy sauce
1 cup (250ml) chicken stock

1 Using a meat mallet, gently pound chicken between sheets of plastic wrap until 1cm thick.
2 Dip chicken in egg white. Coat in flour; shake off excess flour.
3 Heat butter and oil in large frying pan; cook chicken, in batches, until browned and cooked through. Drain on absorbent paper.
4 Blend cornflour and sugar with juice in small saucepan. Add ginger, sauce and stock; bring to a boil. Boil, stirring, until sauce thickens.
5 Slice chicken; serve drizzled with sauce.

on the table in 30 minutes
serves 4 **per serving** 20.5g total fat (6.6g saturated fat); 1982kJ (474 cal); 21.5g carbohydrate; 50.1g protein; 0.8g fibre

Creamy pesto chicken with gnocchi

900g thigh fillets
1 tablespoon olive oil
2 cloves garlic, crushed
2 shallots (50g), chopped finely
100g fresh shiitake mushrooms, sliced thickly
½ cup (125ml) dry white wine
¼ cup (75g) bottled sun-dried tomato pesto
300ml light cream
⅓ cup coarsely chopped fresh basil
625g potato gnocchi

1 Cut each fillet into thirds. Heat oil in large frying pan; cook chicken, in batches, until cooked through. Remove; cover to keep warm.
2 Add garlic, shallot and mushroom to same pan; cook, stirring, 2 minutes. Stir in wine; simmer, uncovered, until liquid is almost evaporated. Stir in pesto and cream; bring to a boil. Remove from heat; stir in basil.
3 Cook gnocchi, in large saucepan of boiling water, uncovered, until gnocchi are just tender and float to the surface; drain.
4 Divide chicken and gnocchi among serving plates; drizzle with creamy pesto sauce.

on the table in 35 minutes
serves 4 **per serving** 49.2g total fat (20.9g saturated fat); 3678kJ (880 cal); 52.1g carbohydrate; 52.9g protein; 5g fibre

Chicken with parsley and lemon

8 thigh fillets (880g)
⅓ cup (50g) plain flour
1 tablespoon olive oil
20g butter
1 cup chopped fresh flat-leaf parsley
2 tablespoons lemon juice
350g baby green beans
polenta
3 cups (750ml) hot water
1 cup (250ml) chicken stock
1 cup (170g) instant polenta
20g butter
½ cup (40g) grated parmesan cheese

1 Toss chicken in flour; shake away excess flour.
2 Heat oil and butter in large frying pan; cook chicken, uncovered, until browned and cooked through. Add parsley and juice; stir to coat chicken.
3 Make polenta.
4 Boil, steam or microwave beans until just tender; drain.
5 Serve chicken with polenta and beans.
polenta combine the hot water and stock in large saucepan, bring to a boil; reduce heat to a simmer. Gradually whisk in polenta and cook, uncovered, stirring frequently, about 5 minutes or until mixture is thick and soft. Stir in butter and parmesan.

on the table in 30 minutes
serves 4 **per serving** 33.1g total fat (13.1g saturated fat); 2847kJ (681 cal); 41.2g carbohydrate; 52.6g protein; 4.8g fibre

Chicken with garden herbs and roast tomato

4 breast fillets (800g)
¼ cup finely chopped fresh chives
¼ cup finely chopped fresh oregano
2 cloves garlic, crushed
1 tablespoon olive oil
500g cherry tomatoes
⅓ cup (80ml) sweet chilli sauce
250g asparagus, trimmed

1 Preheat oven to 180°C/160°C fan-forced.
2 Combine chicken, herbs, garlic and oil in large bowl.
3 Cook chicken mixture in large oiled frying pan until browned. Place chicken in shallow baking dish with combined tomatoes and sauce.
4 Bake, uncovered, about 15 minutes or until chicken is cooked through.
5 Boil, steam or microwave asparagus until just tender.
6 Serve chicken with tomatoes and asparagus.

on the table in 35 minutes
serves 4 **per serving** 9.9g total fat (2.0g saturated fat); 1325kJ (317 cal); 7.5g carbohydrate; 47.2g protein; 3.9g fibre

Sweet chilli chicken with rice

2cm piece fresh ginger (10g), grated
2 cloves garlic, crushed
1 tablespoon finely chopped fresh lemon grass
¼ cup (60ml) sweet chilli sauce
¼ cup (60ml) lime juice
¾ cup coarsely chopped fresh coriander
4 breast fillets (800g)
2 cups (400g) long-grain white rice
¾ cup (180ml) chicken stock
2 teaspoons cornflour

1 Combine ginger, garlic, lemon grass, sauce, juice and a third of the coriander with chicken in large bowl.
2 Boil, steam or microwave rice until just tender; drain, then stir in remaining coriander.
3 Drain chicken over large bowl; reserve marinade. Cook chicken in large oiled frying pan until browned and cooked through; slice chicken thickly.
4 Blend 2 tablespoons of the stock with cornflour in small jug until smooth. Combine remaining stock, cornflour mixture and reserved marinade in medium saucepan; stir until sauce boils and thickens slightly.
5 Serve chicken on rice; drizzle with sauce.

on the table in 30 minutes
serves 4 **per serving** 5.8g total fat (1.5g saturated fat); 2558kJ (312 cal); 84.2g carbohydrate; 52.9g protein; 1.1g fibre

Chicken pitta pockets

8 tenderloins (600g)
2 teaspoons seasoned salt
2 teaspoons olive oil
1 medium brown onion (150g), sliced thinly
¼ cup (75g) mayonnaise
2 teaspoons water
2 teaspoons wholegrain mustard
4 pitta pocket bread
4 green oak leaf lettuce leaves
8 pieces pickled sliced cucumber, drained
2 small egg tomatoes (120g), sliced thinly

1 Combine chicken and salt in medium bowl.
2 Heat oil in large frying pan; cook onion, stirring, until soft. Remove from pan; keep warm.
3 Cook chicken in same pan, until browned and cooked through.
4 Combine mayonnaise, the water and mustard in small bowl.
5 Trim each pitta to open. Fill with lettuce, cucumber, chicken, tomato, onion and mayonnaise mixture.

on the table in 20 minutes
serves 4 **per serving** 17.6g total fat (3.6g saturated fat); 1814kJ (434 cal); 29.7g carbohydrate; 37.2g protein; 3.3g fibre

Rice with chicken and soy

4 dried shiitake mushrooms
500g breast fillets, sliced thinly
2cm piece fresh ginger (10g), grated
2 tablespoons soy sauce
½ teaspoon sesame oil
½ teaspoon cornflour
½ teaspoon white sugar
1 teaspoon chiense cooking wine
1 tablespoon water
1½ cups (300g) jasmine rice
2 cups (500ml) water, extra
1 chinese sausage (lup chong), sliced thinly
2 green onions, sliced thinly

1 Place mushrooms in small heatproof bowl, cover with boiling water, stand about 10 minutes or until tender; drain. Discard stems; slice mushrooms thinly.
2 Meanwhile, combine chicken, ginger, sauce, oil, cornflour, sugar, wine and water in large bowl.
3 Rinse rice under cold water until water runs clear.
4 Place rice and extra water in large saucepan; bring to a boil. Reduce heat to low; cook, covered tightly, for 10 minutes. Do not remove lid or stir during cooking.
5 Drain chicken; reserve marinade. Place chicken, sausage and mushrooms on rice; cook, covered tightly, about 5 minutes or until chicken is cooked through.
6 Place reserved marinade in small saucepan, bring to a boil; simmer 1 minute.
7 Drizzle sauce over chicken and rice; sprinkle with onions. Stir until combined.

on the table in 35 minutes
serves 4 **per serving** 12.9g total fat (2.1g saturated fat); 1626kJ (389 cal); 27.1g carbohydrate; 39.1g protein; 3.1g fibre
tip use dry sherry instead of chinese cooking wine, if desired.

Chicken and ham patties

1kg mince
250g sliced ham, chopped finely
2 tablespoons chopped fresh coriander
1 clove garlic, crushed
3 green onions, chopped finely
1 cup (70g) stale breadcrumbs
¼ cup (60ml) olive oil
dipping sauce
2 tablespoons soy sauce
1 tablespoon sweet chilli sauce

1 Make dipping sauce.
2 Combine all ingredients, except the oil, in large bowl. Shape ¼ cups of mixture into flat patties.
3 Heat oil in medium frying pan; cook patties, in batches, until browned both sides and cooked through.
4 Serve patties with dipping sauce and rocket leaves, if desired.
dipping sauce combine ingredients in small bowl.

on the table in 25 minutes
serves 6 per serving 24.6g total fat (5.9g saturated fat); 1772kJ (424 cal); 8.8g carbohydrate; 41.4g protein; 0.8g fibre

Pollo parmigiana

2 breast fillets (400g)
2 tablespoons plain flour
1 egg
1 tablespoon milk
1 cup (70g) stale breadcrumbs
¼ cup (60ml) vegetable oil
⅓ cup (85g) bottled tomato pasta sauce, warmed
4 slices leg ham (185g)
100g gruyère cheese, grated coarsely

1 Preheat grill.
2 Split chicken fillets in half horizontally. Toss chicken in flour; shake away excess. Dip chicken pieces, one at a time, in combined egg and milk, then in breadcrumbs.
3 Heat oil in large frying pan; shallow-fry chicken, in batches, until browned and cooked through. Drain on absorbent paper.
4 Place chicken on oven tray; spoon pasta sauce over chicken, top with ham and cheese. Place under grill until cheese melts. Serve with a baby rocket and parmesan cheese salad, if desired.

on the table in 30 minutes
serves 4 **per serving** 28.6g total fat (8.7g saturated fat); 2103kJ (503 cal); 17.9g carbohydrate; 43.3g protein; 1.3g fibre

Chicken with creamy herb sauce, capsicums, beans and garlic

4 breast fillets (800g)
2 tablespoons olive oil
4 green onions, chopped
2 teaspoons cornflour
1½ cups (375ml) chicken stock
80g packet cheese with garlic and herbs, crumbled
1 tablespoon chopped fresh flat-leaf parsley
1 tablespoon chopped fresh chives
20g butter
200g green beans, halved
1 clove garlic, crushed
1 medium green capsicum (200g), sliced
1 medium red capsicum (200g), sliced

1 Cut chicken in half horizontally to form thin fillets.
2 Heat oil in large frying pan; cook chicken, in batches, over high heat until browned both sides and just cooked through. Remove from pan; cover to keep warm.
3 Add onion to same pan; cook, stirring, until soft. Stir in combined cornflour and stock; stir until mixture boils and thickens. Add cheese; stir until melted. Stir in herbs.
4 Melt butter in frying pan; cook beans, stirring, until almost tender. Add garlic and capsicum; cook, stirring, until tender.
5 Serve chicken with vegetables, sauce and bread, if desired.

on the table in 35 minutes
serves 4 **per serving** 23.8g total fat (8.8g saturated fat); 1944kJ (465 cal); 6.7g carbohydrate; 54.6g protein; 2.8g fibre

Chicken burgers

500g mince
1 medium zucchini (120g), grated coarsely
1 medium carrot (120g), grated coarsely
2 tablespoons plain flour
2 teaspoons cajun seasoning
4 wholemeal bread rolls
2 medium tomatoes (300g), seeded, chopped finely
1 tablespoon chopped fresh chives
2 teaspoons olive oil
4 large lettuce leaves
⅓ cup (85g) sour cream
¼ teaspoon hot paprika

1 Using hands, combine chicken, zucchini, carrot, flour and seasoning in large bowl; shape mixture into four patties. Cook patties in large heated oiled frying pan until browned both sides and cooked through.
2 Split rolls in half; toast cut sides until browned lightly. Combine tomato, chives and oil in small bowl.
3 To serve, sandwich burgers, lettuce, tomato mixture and combined sour cream and paprika between roll halves.

on the table in 25 minutes
serves 4 **per serving** 23.6g total fat (9.0g saturated fat); 2320kJ (555 cal); 46.4g carbohydrate; 35.3g protein; 7.9g fibre

Satay chicken with yogurt

750g tenderloins
525g bottled satay sauce
1 tablespoon olive oil
2 large brown onions (400g), cut into wedges
250g cherry tomatoes, halved
⅓ cup shredded fresh basil
200g yogurt
2 tablespoons sweet chilli sauce

1 Combine chicken and ½ cup (125ml) of the satay sauce in large bowl; stand 5 minutes.
2 Cook chicken, in batches, in large heated oiled frying pan until cooked through. Cover to keep warm.
3 Heat oil in same pan; cook onion, stirring, until soft. Add remaining satay sauce, tomatoes and basil; cook, stirring, about 5 minutes or until heated through.
4 Return chicken to pan; stir to coat with satay sauce mixture. Serve chicken with combined yogurt and sweet chilli sauce.

on the table in 30 minutes
serves 4 **per serving** 42.3g total fat (12.5g saturated fat); 3294kJ (788 cal); 45.1g carbohydrate; 54.0g protein; 6.3g fibre

Chicken marsala

7 canned anchovy fillets, drained, chopped finely
1 tablespoon drained capers, chopped finely
1 tablespoon chopped fresh parsley
1 clove garlic, chopped roughly
1 tablespoon olive oil
4 breast fillets (800g)
125g mozzarella cheese
¼ cup (60ml) marsala
1 cup (250ml) chicken stock
½ cup (125ml) cream

1 Combine anchovy, caper, parsley and garlic in small bowl.
2 Heat oil in large frying pan; cook chicken until browned both sides.
Remove from pan.
3 Cut mozzarella into 4 even slices. Spread anchovy mixture evenly on
top of chicken; top with cheese.
4 Return chicken to pan; cook, covered, about 10 minutes or until
chicken is cooked through and cheese is melting. Remove from pan;
cover to keep warm.
5 Add marsala and stock to same pan, bring to a boil; simmer, uncovered,
about 5 minutes or until reduced by one-third. Stir in cream; simmer,
uncovered, further 5 minutes or until thickened slightly. Spoon sauce
over chicken. Serve with pasta, if desired.

on the table in 35 minutes
serves 4 **per serving** 31.3g total fat (15.7g saturated fat); 2445kJ
(585 cal); 7.7g carbohydrate; 62.0g protein; 0.2g fibre

Pan-fried green peppercorn chicken

8 thigh cutlets (1.3kg)
¼ cup (60g) wholegrain mustard
2 tablespoons drained green peppercorns, chopped
2 cloves garlic, crushed
2 tablespoons lemon juice
¼ cup chopped fresh chives
¼ cup (60ml) olive oil
1 small white onion (80g), chopped finely

1 Remove and discard skin from chicken. Combine chicken, mustard, peppercorns, garlic, juice, chives and 2 tablespoons of the oil in large bowl.
2 Heat remaining oil in large frying pan; cook onion, stirring, until soft.
3 Add chicken to pan; cook, brushing occasionally with peppercorn mixture, until chicken is browned both sides and cooked through.

on the table in 30 minutes
serves 4 **per serving** 29.3g total fat (6.6g saturated fat); 1839kJ (440 cal); 3.8g carbohydrate; 40.4g protein; 1.2g fibre

Chicken in red wine and tomato sauce

30g butter
2 tablespoons olive oil
2 medium white onions (300g), sliced thinly
2 cloves garlic, crushed
750g thigh fillets, halved
250g button mushrooms, sliced thinly
2 x 400g cans tomatoes
¼ cup (60ml) tomato paste
¼ cup (60ml) dry red wine
2 teaspoons brown sugar
1 teaspoon cracked black peppercorns
½ cup (125ml) chicken stock
¼ cup coarsely chopped fresh basil

1 Heat butter and oil in large frying pan; cook onion and garlic, stirring, until onion is soft. Add chicken; cook until cooked through.
2 Stir in mushrooms, undrained crushed tomatoes, paste, wine, sugar, peppercorns and stock; bring to a boil. Reduce heat, simmer, uncovered, until sauce has thickened slightly. Remove from heat; stir in basil.

on the table in 30 minutes
serves 4 **per serving** 29.7g total fat (9.5g saturated fat); 2128kJ (509 cal); 14.8g carbohydrate; 41.0g protein; 6.1g fibre

curries

Thai green curry

500g breast fillets, sliced thickly
1 large brown onion (200g), chopped coarsely
2 cloves garlic, crushed
4cm piece fresh ginger (20g), grated
10cm stick (20g) fresh lemon grass, chopped finely
2 tablespoons green curry paste
1 tablespoon peanut oil
¾ cup (180ml) chicken stock
1⅔ cups (400ml) coconut milk
2 tablespoons lime juice
230g can sliced bamboo shoots, drained
300g fresh baby corn, halved
½ cup coarsely chopped fresh coriander

1 Combine chicken, onion, garlic, ginger, lemon grass and paste in medium bowl.
2 Heat oil in wok; cook chicken mixture, in batches, until chicken is just browned.
3 Return chicken mixture to wok with stock, coconut milk and juice; cook, uncovered, about 5 minutes or until curry mixture thickens slightly and chicken is cooked through.
4 Reduce heat. Add bamboo shoots, corn and coriander; stir until heated through. Serve with steamed rice, if desired.

on the table in 25 minutes
serves 4 **per serving** 33.0g total fat (20.3g saturated fat); 2274kJ (544 cal); 21.7g carbohydrate; 36.4g protein; 8.3g fibre

Lentil and pumpkin vindaloo

¾ cup (150g) red lentils
500g pumpkin, chopped coarsely
700g thigh fillets, sliced thickly
1 medium white onion (150g), chopped coarsely
4cm piece fresh ginger (20g), grated
2 cloves garlic, crushed
1 tablespoon peanut oil
¼ cup (75g) vindaloo curry paste
1⅔ cups (400ml) coconut cream
250g baby spinach leaves

1 Cook lentils in large saucepan of boiling water, uncovered, until just tender; drain. Boil, steam or microwave pumpkin until just tender; drain.
2 Combine chicken, onion, ginger and garlic in large bowl.
3 Heat oil in wok; stir-fry chicken mixture, in batches, until chicken is just browned.
4 Stir curry paste in wok until fragrant. Return chicken mixture to wok with lentils, pumpkin and coconut cream; cook, stirring, until sauce thickens slightly and chicken is cooked through.
5 Remove from heat. Add spinach; toss gently until spinach just wilts.

on the table in 30 minutes
serves 4 **per serving** 44.7g total fat (23.5g saturated fat); 3064kJ (733 cal); 28.6g carbohydrate; 48.8g protein; 12.5g fibre
tip you can substitute any bottled curry paste for the fiery vindaloo.

Chicken and bean madras

1½ cups (300g) basmati rice
1 tablespoon peanut oil
1 large white onion (200g), sliced thinly
700g thigh fillets, sliced thinly
¼ cup (75g) madras curry paste
200g green beans, chopped coarsely
½ cup (125ml) chicken stock
1 tablespoon tomato paste

1 Cook rice in large saucepan of boiling water, uncovered, until just tender; drain.
2 Meanwhile, heat oil in wok; cook onion and chicken, in batches, until chicken is just browned.
3 Stir curry paste in wok until fragrant. Return chicken mixture to wok with beans, stock and tomato paste; stir until sauce thickens slightly and chicken is cooked through. Serve with rice.

on the table in 25 minutes
serves 4 **per serving** 23.7g total fat (5.4g saturated fat); 2709kJ (648 cal); 65.4g carbohydrate; 40.8g protein; 4.7g fibre
tips you can substitute jasmine rice for the basmati rice. The curry paste we used contained whole and partially chopped star anise, giving this recipe a distinctively spicy flavour.

Indonesian chicken curry

1 tablespoon peanut oil
750g thigh fillets, chopped coarsely
1 large brown onion (200g), sliced thickly
1 fresh small red thai chilli, chopped finely
2 cloves garlic, crushed
4cm piece fresh ginger (20g), grated
1 tablespoon finely chopped macadamia nuts
1 tablespoon ground coriander
1 teaspoon ground cumin
½ teaspoon ground fennel
1 cinnamon stick
3¼ cups (800ml) coconut cream
1 tablespoon lemon juice

1 Heat half of the oil in wok; cook chicken, in batches, until browned all over and cooked through.
2 Heat remaining oil in wok; cook onion, chilli, garlic and ginger, stirring, until onion softens. Add nuts and spices; cook, stirring, until fragrant.
3 Return chicken to wok with coconut cream and juice; bring to a boil. Reduce heat, simmer, uncovered, 5 minutes or until sauce thickens slightly. Serve with steamed rice and sprinkled with sliced chilli, if desired.

on the table in 30 minutes
serves 4 **per serving** 61.9g total fat (41.6g saturated fat); 3181kJ (761 cal); 11.0g carbohydrate; 39.8g protein; 4.7g fibre
tip this coconut chicken curry is the ideal choice for people who don't like fiery curries.

Butter chicken

80g butter
1 medium brown onion (150g), chopped finely
3 cloves garlic, crushed
3 teaspoons sweet paprika
2 teaspoons garam masala
2 teaspoons ground coriander
½ teaspoon chilli powder
1 cinnamon stick
2 tablespoons white vinegar
425g can tomato puree
¾ cup (180ml) chicken stock
1 tablespoon tomato paste
750g thigh fillets, quartered
1 cup (250ml) cream
½ cup (140g) yogurt

1 Melt butter in large saucepan; cook onion, garlic and spices, stirring, until onion softens.
2 Add vinegar, puree, stock and paste; bring to a boil. Reduce heat, simmer, uncovered, stirring occasionally, for 10 minutes.
3 Add chicken to pan with cream and yogurt; bring to a boil. Reduce heat, simmer, uncovered, about 10 minutes or until chicken is cooked through.

on the table in 30 minutes
serves 4 **per serving** 58.1g total fat (22.7g saturated fat); 3068kJ (734 cal); 12.3g carbohydrate; 40.7g protein; 3.1g fibre
tip in India, this dish is often made using leftover tandoori chicken pieces; it can also be made using chicken breast fillets, if you prefer.

baked

Oven-baked parmesan chicken

1 tablespoon plain flour
2 eggs, beaten lightly
2 cups (140g) stale breadcrumbs
⅓ cup (25g) coarsely grated parmesan cheese
2 tablespoons finely chopped fresh flat-leaf parsley
12 tenderloins (900g)
1 cup firmly packed fresh basil leaves
½ cup (125ml) olive oil
¼ cup (60ml) lemon juice
1 clove garlic, quartered
¾ cup (120g) kalamata olives, seeded
200g curly endive
40g baby rocket leaves

1 Preheat oven to 220°C/200°C fan-forced.
2 Combine flour and egg in medium bowl. In another medium bowl combine breadcrumbs, cheese and parsley. Coat chicken, one piece at a time, first in flour mixture then in breadcrumb mixture. Place chicken, in single layer, on oiled oven tray; bake, uncovered, about 15 minutes or until chicken is lightly browned and cooked through.
3 Meanwhile, blend or process basil, oil, juice and garlic until well combined.
4 Serve chicken with combined olives, endive and rocket; drizzle with basil dressing.

on the table in 30 minutes
serves 4 **per serving** 38.9g total fat (7.4g saturated fat); 3093kJ (740 cal); 34.1g carbohydrate; 61.6g protein; 3.7g fibre

Peri peri chicken

2 tablespoons lemon juice
1 tablespoon olive oil
6 fresh small red thai chillies, chopped finely
2 teaspoons brown sugar
1 teaspoon sweet paprika
2 cloves garlic, crushed
2 teaspoons finely chopped fresh rosemary
2 teaspoons sea salt
4 maryland pieces (1.4kg)

1 Preheat oven to 220°C/200°C fan-forced.
2 Combine juice, oil, chilli, sugar, paprika, garlic, rosemary and salt in large bowl.
3 Make deep diagonal cuts in chicken pieces. Rub spice mixture all over chicken; stand 10 minutes.
4 Place chicken in single layer on oven tray; bake, uncovered, 20 minutes or until cooked through.

on the table in 35 minutes
serves 4 **per serving** 37.2g total fat (11.1g saturated fat); 2128kJ (509 cal); 2.1g carbohydrate; 42.4g protein; 0.3g fibre

Peanut-crusted thai chicken with cucumber salad

1 cup (150g) roasted unsalted peanuts
¼ cup (75g) red curry paste
1 tablespoon kecap manis
½ cup (125ml) coconut milk
1 cup coarsely chopped fresh coriander
4 breast fillets (800g)
1 telegraph cucumber (400g)
2 cups (160g) bean sprouts
⅓ cup coarsely chopped fresh mint
1 medium red onion (170g), halved, sliced thinly
1 teaspoon fish sauce
2 tablespoons sweet chilli sauce
1 tablespoon lime juice
1 tablespoon peanut oil

1 Preheat oven to 200°C/180°C fan-forced.
2 Blend or process peanuts, paste, kecap manis, coconut milk and half of the coriander until just combined.
3 Place chicken, in single layer, on oiled oven tray; spread peanut mixture on each piece. bake, uncovered, about 20 minutes or until chicken is cooked through. Remove chicken from oven; cover, stand 5 minutes, slice thickly.
4 Meanwhile, cut cucumber in half lengthways. Remove and discard seeds; slice thinly. Combine cucumber in large bowl with sprouts, mint, onion and remaining coriander.
5 Place sauces, juice and oil in screw-top jar; shake well. Pour dressing over cucumber salad; toss gently to combine. Serve chicken topped with salad.

on the table in 30 minutes
serves 4 **per serving** 39.7g total fat (10.4g saturated fat); 2780kJ (665 cal); 13.6g carbohydrate; 59.4g protein; 8.9g fibre

Tandoori drumettes with cucumber raita

2 cups (400g) jasmine rice
12 drumettes (960g)
2 tablespoons tandoori paste
400g yogurt
1 lebanese cucumber (130g), seeded, chopped finely
1 tablespoon finely chopped fresh mint
1 teaspoon ground cumin

1 Preheat oven to 220°C/200°C fan-forced.
2 Cook rice in large saucepan of boiling water, uncovered, until just tender; drain.
3 Meanwhile, combine chicken, paste and half of the yogurt in large bowl. Place chicken, in single layer, on wire oven rack over baking dish; bake, uncovered, about 20 minutes or until chicken is browned all over and cooked through.
4 Combine remaining yogurt with cucumber, mint and cumin in small bowl. Serve rice topped with tandoori chicken and cucumber raita.

on the table in 25 minutes
serves 4 **per serving** 21.9g total fat (7.0g saturated fat); 2888kJ (691 cal); 85.4g carbohydrate; 35.1g protein; 3.9g fibre
tips raita is a fresh yogurt salad that goes extremely well with spicy Indian dishes. Drumettes are in fact wings trimmed to resemble drumsticks; in some areas, this name is used (along with lovely legs) when describing pared-back and trimmed drumsticks. You can use either in this recipe.

Malay chicken

1 tablespoon ground coriander
1 tablespoon ground cumin
1 tablespoon fennel seeds
1 teaspoon ground cinnamon
½ teaspoon ground turmeric
2 fresh small red thai chillies, chopped finely
½ teaspoon tamarind concentrate
2 cloves garlic, crushed
5cm stick (10g) fresh lemon grass, chopped finely
2 teaspoons palm sugar
1 tablespoon peanut oil
½ cup (125ml) coconut cream
8 thigh cutlets (1.3kg)

1 Preheat oven to 220°C/200°C fan-forced.
2 Combine spices, chilli, tamarind, garlic, lemon grass, sugar, oil and coconut cream in large bowl; stir until mixture forms a paste.
3 Add chicken to bowl; stir to coat in paste.
4 Place chicken on wire rack in large shallow baking dish; bake about 20 minutes. Cover with foil; bake further 10 minutes, or until chicken is cooked through.

on the table in 35 minutes
serves 4 **per serving** 26.1g total fat (11.0g saturated fat); 1689kJ (404 cal); 3.0g carbohydrate; 39.8g protein; 0.8g fibre

Chicken tikka drumettes

12 drumettes (960g)
⅓ cup (100g) tikka paste
½ cup (140g) yogurt
2 cups (400g) jasmine rice
12 small pappadums
¼ cup coarsely chopped fresh coriander
⅓ cup (110g) mild lime pickle

1 Preheat oven to 200°C/180°C fan-forced.
2 Combine chicken with combined paste and 2 tablespoons of the yogurt in large bowl.
3 Place chicken, in single layer, on wire rack in large baking dish; bake, uncovered, about 20 minutes or until chicken is browned and cooked through.
4 Meanwhile, cook rice in large saucepan of boiling water, uncovered, until just tender; drain. Cover to keep warm.
5 Place three pappadums around edge of microwave oven turntable. Cook on HIGH (100%) about 30 seconds or until puffed. Repeat with remaining pappadums.
6 Combine coriander and remaining yogurt in small bowl. Serve chicken on rice drizzled with yogurt mixture; accompany with lime pickle and pappadums.

on the table in 35 minutes
serves 4 **per serving** 22.7g total fat (5.4g saturated fat); 3148kJ (753 cal); 95.3g carbohydrate; 38.1g protein; 5.8g fibre
tip pappadums can also be deep-fried in vegetable oil.

Sticky barbecue wings

2 cups (400g) long-grain white rice
12 wings (1kg)
¼ cup (60ml) barbecue sauce
¼ cup (60ml) plum sauce
1 tablespoon worcestershire sauce

1 Preheat oven to 220°C/200°C fan-forced.
2 Cook rice in large saucepan of boiling water, uncovered, until just tender; drain. Cover to keep warm.
3 Meanwhile, cut wing tips from chicken; cut wings in half at joint.
4 Combine chicken with combined sauces in large bowl. Place chicken, in single layer, in large oiled baking dish; baked, uncovered, about 20 minutes or until chicken is cooked through. Serve chicken with rice.

on the table in 30 minutes
serves 4 **per serving** 9.0g total fat (2.8g saturated fat); 2700kJ (646 cal); 96.1g carbohydrate; 42.9g protein; 1.1g fibre

Chicken, asparagus and potatoes in garlic cream sauce

500g kipfler potatoes, halved lengthways
1 teaspoon cracked black pepper
1 tablespoon olive oil
4 breast fillets (800g)
400g asparagus, trimmed
6 slices prosciutto (90g), chopped coarsely
1 clove garlic, crushed
½ cup (125ml) dry white wine
2 tablespoons wholegrain mustard
300ml cream
¼ cup coarsely chopped fresh chives

1 Preheat oven to 220°C/200°C fan-forced.

2 Combine potato, pepper and oil in large bowl. Place potato, in single layer, on oiled oven tray; bake, uncovered, 20 minutes or until browned.

3 Meanwhile, heat large lightly oiled frying pan; cook chicken, in batches, until browned both sides. Place chicken, in single layer, on oven tray; bake, uncovered, with potatoes about 10 minutes or until cooked through.

4 Remove chicken and potato from oven; cover, stand 5 minutes. Slice chicken thickly.

5 Boil, steam or microwave asparagus until just tender; drain. Cover to keep warm.

6 Cook prosciutto in same frying pan, stirring, until just crisp. Remove from pan; cover to keep warm. Add garlic to pan; cook, stirring, over low heat until fragrant. Add wine; bring to a boil. Boil, stirring, until reduced to about 2 tablespoons. Add mustard and cream; bring to a boil. Boil, stirring, until mixture thickens slightly. Stir in chives.

7 Divide asparagus among serving plates; top with potato, half of the prosciutto, chicken, sauce, then remaining prosciutto.

on the table in 35 minutes
serves 4 **per serving** 43.1g total fat (23.6g saturated fat); 3018kJ (722 cal); 20.8g carbohydrate; 56.2g protein; 4.2g fibre
tips kipfler potatoes, small and finger-shaped, have a nutty flavour and are great baked or in salads. You will need two bunches of asparagus for this recipe.

Satay drumettes

12 drumettes (960g)
¼ cup (60ml) kecap manis
2 cups (400g) jasmine rice
¾ cup (210g) crunchy peanut butter
⅔ cup (160ml) chicken stock
2 tablespoons sweet chilli sauce
1 tablespoon light soy sauce
1 tablespoon lemon juice
1 cup (250ml) coconut milk

1 Preheat oven to 220°C/200°C fan-forced.
2 Place chicken, in single layer, in large shallow oiled baking dish; brush chicken all over with kecap manis. Bake, uncovered, about 20 minutes or until chicken is cooked through.
3 Meanwhile, cook rice in large saucepan of boiling water, uncovered, until just tender; drain. Cover to keep warm.
4 Combine peanut butter, stock, sauces, juice and coconut milk in medium saucepan; bring to a boil. Reduce heat, simmer, uncovered, 5 minutes.
5 Serve rice and chicken drizzled with satay sauce.

on the table in 30 minutes
serves 4 **per serving** 49.9g total fat (15.9g saturated fat); 4222kJ (1010 cal); 90.1g carbohydrate; 46.9g protein; 7.0g fibre
tip you can also cook the drumettes on a grill or barbecue. Drumettes are in fact wings trimmed to resemble drumsticks; in some areas, this name is used (along with lovely legs) when describing pared-back and trimmed drumsticks. You can use either in this recipe.

Lemon grass chicken

8 lovely legs (960g)
10cm stick (20g) fresh lemon grass, chopped finely
4 spring onions (100g), chopped finely
2 teaspoons fish sauce
1 teaspoon sambal oelek
1 teaspoon white sugar
1 tablespoon peanut oil

1 Preheat oven to 220°C/200°C fan-forced.
2 Combine chicken and remaining ingredients in baking dish.
3 Bake, uncovered, about 30 minutes or until chicken is cooked through, turning chicken once during cooking.

on the table in 35 minutes
serves 4 **per serving** 14.2g total fat (3.6g saturated fat); 1058kJ (253 cal); 2.3g carbohydrate; 30.0g protein; 0.6g fibre
tip you can use any cut of chicken you wish in this recipe. Lovely legs are trimmed, skinned chicken drumsticks.

Light and spicy crumbed chicken

12 tenderloins (900g)
⅓ cup (50g) plain flour
2 egg whites, beaten lightly
⅓ cup (35g) packaged breadcrumbs
⅓ cup (35g) corn flake crumbs
2 teaspoons garlic salt
1 teaspoon lemon pepper

1 Preheat oven to 220°C/200°C fan-forced.
2 Toss chicken in flour; shake away excess flour. Coat chicken in egg whites, then in combined breadcrumbs, corn flake crumbs, salt and pepper. Cover; refrigerate 10 minutes.
3 Place chicken in single layer on oven tray; bake, uncovered, 15 minutes or until cooked through.

on the table in 35 minutes
serves 4 **per serving** 5.7g total fat (1.4g saturated fat); 1542kJ (369 cal); 22.2g carbohydrate; 55.8g protein; 1.1g fibre

Cajun chicken with creole rice

½ teaspoon salt
2 teaspoons onion powder
3 teaspoons sweet paprika
1 teaspoon freshly ground black pepper
½ teaspoon chilli powder
4 breast fillets (800g)
creole rice
1 tablespoon olive oil
1 medium brown onion (150g), chopped finely
3 cloves garlic, crushed
1 medium green capsicum (200g), chopped finely
1 teaspoon chilli powder
1 teaspoon ground cumin
1 teaspoon ground cinnamon
1 cup (200g) long-grain white rice
2 cups (500ml) water
2 tablespoons lime juice
¼ cup coarsely chopped fresh coriander
310g can corn kernels, rinsed, drained
420g can red kidney beans, rinsed, drained

1 Preheat oven to 200°C/180°C fan-forced. Oil oven tray.
2 Combine salt and spices in medium bowl; coat chicken, one piece at a time, in spice mixture.
3 Place chicken, in single layer, on tray; bake, uncovered, 20 minutes or until chicken is browned all over and cooked through. Remove chicken from oven; stand 5 minutes, slice thickly.
4 Meanwhile, make creole rice.
5 Serve chicken on rice; drizzle with pan juices, if any.
creole rice heat oil in large saucepan; cook onion and garlic, stirring, until onion softens. Add capsicum and spices; cook, stirring, until fragrant. Stir in rice; add the water, bring to a boil. Reduce heat, simmer, covered, 15 minutes. Add remaining ingredients; stir until heated through.

on the table in 30 minutes
serves 4 **per serving** 10.6g total fat (2.0g saturated fat); 2491kJ
(596 cal); 63.3g carbohydrate; 56.4g protein; 8.2g fibre

takeaway

Each takeaway barbecued chicken we used in this chapter weighed about 900g; when skinned and boned, this results in 3 cups (480g) of shredded meat, or 2½ cups (425g) of coarsely chopped meat.

Chicken salad with sesame dressing

1 large barbecued chicken (900g)
2 medium carrots (240g)
½ small wombok (350g), shredded thickly
6 green onions, sliced thickly
1 cup (80g) bean sprouts
¼ cup firmly packed fresh coriander leaves
sesame dressing
2 cloves garlic, crushed
½ teaspoon sesame oil
2 tablespoons peanut oil
1 tablespoon soy sauce
1 tablespoon lemon juice
1 teaspoon white sugar
1 tablespoon white wine vinegar

1 Cut chicken into eight pieces.
2 Using a vegetable peeler, peel thin strips lengthways from carrots. Combine carrot, wombok, onion, sprouts and coriander; top with chicken.
3 Make sesame dressing; drizzle dressing over salad and chicken.
sesame dressing place ingredients in screw-top jar; shake well.

on the table in 20 minutes
serves 4 **per serving** 19.6g total fat (4.6g saturated fat); 1400kJ (335 cal); 5.2g carbohydrate; 33.3g protein; 3.0g fibre

Pappardelle chicken and creamy mushroom sauce

500g pappardelle pasta
2 tablespoons olive oil
1 clove garlic, crushed
1 small brown onion (80g), chopped finely
250g swiss brown mushrooms, sliced thinly
¾ cup (180ml) cream
2 teaspoons finely chopped fresh rosemary
20g butter
3 cups (480g) shredded cooked chicken
½ cup (60g) coarsely chopped toasted walnuts
¼ cup coarsely chopped fresh flat-leaf parsley
¾ cup (60g) finely grated parmesan cheese

1 Cook pasta in large saucepan of boiling water, uncovered, until just tender; drain. Return to pan.
2 Meanwhile, heat oil in large frying pan; cook garlic and onion, stirring, until onion softens. Add mushroom; cook, stirring, until just tender.
3 Add cream and rosemary to pan; bring to a boil. Reduce heat, simmer, uncovered, until sauce thickens slightly. Add butter; stir until butter melts.
4 Add hot cream sauce, chicken, nuts, parsley and half of the cheese to hot pasta; toss gently to combine. Serve immediately, sprinkled with remaining cheese.

on the table in 30 minutes
serves 4 **per serving** 55.7g total fat (21.5g saturated fat); 4548kJ (1088 cal); 91.5g carbohydrate; 54.9g protein; 9.3g fibre

Chicken wraps

1 large tomato (220g), chopped coarsely
1 medium avocado (320g), chopped coarsely
1 small red onion (100g), chopped coarsely
2 tablespoons chopped fresh coriander
½ cup (130g) bottled medium chunky salsa
3 cups (480g) shredded cooked chicken
8 large flour tortillas

1 Combine tomato, avocado, onion, coriander, salsa and chicken in large bowl.
2 Heat one tortilla in microwave on HIGH (100%) about 20 seconds or until just flexible.
3 Top tortilla with about an eighth of the chicken filling; roll to enclose filling. Repeat with remaining tortillas and chicken filling.

on the table in 20 minutes
serves 4 **per serving** 28.5g total fat (6.4g saturated fat); 2671kJ (639 cal); 53.0g carbohydrate; 39.8g protein; 5.2g fibre

Chicken pasta salad with roasted capsicum, fetta and walnut

300g frilled pasta shells
270g jar char-grilled capsicum in oil
150g fetta cheese, chopped coarsely
2½ cups (425g) coarsely chopped cooked chicken
⅓ cup (35g) toasted walnuts, chopped coarsely
1 cup loosely packed fresh basil leaves
¼ cup (60ml) red wine vinegar
1 clove garlic, crushed
2 teaspoons wholegrain mustard

1 Cook pasta in large saucepan of boiling water, uncovered, until just tender; drain. Rinse under cold running water; drain.
2 Drain capsicum, reserving ⅓ cup of the capsicum oil; chop capsicum coarsely. Combine capsicum and pasta in large bowl with cheese, chicken, walnuts and basil.
3 Place reserved oil with vinegar, garlic and mustard in screw-top jar; shake well. Drizzle dressing over chicken mixture; toss gently to combine.

on the table in 20 minutes
serves 4 **per serving** 43.7g total fat (11.5g saturated fat); 3289kJ (787 cal); 53.4g carbohydrate; 43.3g protein; 4.0g fibre
tip you can substitute goat cheese or any soft, crumbly cheese for the fetta in this recipe.

Chicken noodle soup

2 teaspoons olive oil
1 medium leek (350g), chopped coarsely
1 large carrot (180g), chopped coarsely
2 trimmed celery stalks (200g), chopped coarsely
1 clove garlic, crushed
1.5 litres (6 cups) chicken stock
2 cups (320g) shredded cooked chicken
50g rice vermicelli noodles
2 tablespoons chopped fresh flat-leaf parsley

1 Heat oil in large saucepan; cook leek, carrot, celery and garlic, stirring, until leek is soft.
2 Stir in stock, bring to a boil; simmer, covered, about 20 minutes or until vegetables are tender.
3 Stir in chicken and noodles; simmer, uncovered, stirring, until noodles are tender. Stir in parsley.

on the table in 35 minutes
serves 6 **per serving** 6.8g total fat (1.9g saturated fat); 677kJ (162 cal); 6.8g carbohydrate; 17.2g protein; 2.6g fibre
tip you can substitute rice noodles or wheat noodles for the rice vermicelli in this recipe.

Chicken nachos

1 tablespoon vegetable oil
1 medium brown onion (150g), chopped finely
425g can mexican-style beans, drained
3 cups (480g) shredded cooked chicken
390g jar mild nachos topping sauce
230g packet corn chips
2 cups (220g) grated pizza cheese
1 medium avocado (320g), mashed coarsely
⅔ cup (160g) sour cream

1 Heat oil in medium frying pan; cook onion, stirring, until softened.
Stir in beans, chicken and sauce; bring to a boil. Reduce heat, simmer,
uncovered, about 3 minutes or until mixture thickens slightly.
2 Divide corn chips among four microwave-safe serving dishes;
top each with cheese. Microwave, one plate at a time, uncovered,
on HIGH (100%) about 1 minute or until cheese has melted.
3 Top plates of corn chips and cheese with equal amounts of chicken
mixture, avocado and sour cream.

on the table in 25 minutes
serves 4 **per serving** 70.4g total fat (30.8g saturated fat); 4682kJ
(1120 cal); 53.9g carbohydrate; 61.4g protein; 16.1g fibre
tip pizza cheese is a convenient blend of coarsely grated processed
cheddar, mozzarella and parmesan cheeses available from supermarkets.

Teriyaki rice paper rolls

1 cup (160g) shredded cooked chicken
1 small carrot (70g), grated coarsely
1 small red capsicum (150g), sliced thinly
100g fresh shiitake mushrooms, sliced thinly
50g snow pea tendrils
2 tablespoons coarsely chopped fresh coriander
2 tablespoons teriyaki sauce
1 tablespoon sweet chilli sauce
12 x 22cm rice paper rounds

1 Combine chicken, carrot, capsicum, mushroom, tendrils, coriander and sauces in large bowl.
2 Place one sheet of rice paper in medium bowl of warm water until just softened; lift sheet carefully from water, place on board covered with a tea towel.
3 Place some of the filling in the centre of sheet; fold in sides, roll top to bottom to enclose filling. Repeat with remaining rice paper sheets and filling.

on the table in 35 minutes
serves 4 **per serving** 3.6g total fat (1.0g saturated fat); 623kJ (149 cal); 13.7g carbohydrate; 14.0g protein; 2.8g fibre
tip serve with sweet chilli sauce or soy sauce.

Chicken with creamy sun-dried tomato sauce

1 tablespoon olive oil
1 medium brown onion (150g), chopped finely
2 teaspoons tomato paste
⅔ cup (100g) drained sun-dried tomatoes, chopped coarsely
¼ cup (60ml) dry white wine
½ cup (125ml) chicken stock
300ml cream
2 tablespoons chopped fresh sage
1 large barbecued chicken (900g), skinned, quartered

1 Heat oil in large frying pan; cook onion, stirring, until lightly browned.
2 Add paste, tomato and wine; cook, uncovered, until liquid is almost evaporated. Add stock, cream and sage; bring to a boil.
3 Add chicken; reduce heat. Simmer, uncovered, until sauce thickens slightly and chicken is heated through. Serve with steamed rice, if desired.

on the table in 25 minutes
serves 4 **per serving** 48.5g total fat (25.0g saturated fat); 2713kJ (649 cal); 13.2g carbohydrate; 36.5g protein; 4.2g fibre

Thai chicken and lychee salad

3 cups (480g) shredded cooked chicken
565g can lychees in syrup, drained, halved, seeded
1 small red onion (100g), sliced thinly
8 green onions, sliced thinly
2 cups (160g) bean sprouts
½ cup firmly packed fresh mint leaves
½ cup firmly packed fresh coriander leaves
dressing
1 teaspoon finely grated lime rind
1 teaspoon sambal oelek
¼ cup (60ml) lime juice
1 teaspoon sesame oil
1 tablespoon brown sugar
2 teaspoons fish sauce

1 Make dressing.
2 Place chicken, lychees, onions, sprouts, mint and coriander in large bowl. Drizzle dressing over salad; toss gently to combine.
dressing place ingredients in screw-top jar; shake well.

on the table in 15 minutes
serves 4 **per serving** 10.6g total fat (2.8g saturated fat); 1400kJ (335 cal); 24.3g carbohydrate; 33.2g protein; 4.0g fibre

Singapore noodles

450g fresh singapore noodles
2 teaspoons sesame oil
2 cloves garlic, crushed
2cm piece fresh ginger (10g), grated
1 medium carrot (120g), cut into matchsticks
250g cooked shelled small prawns
1 tablespoon malaysian curry powder
3 green onions, sliced thinly
1½ cups bean sprouts (120g)
2 tablespoons soy sauce
¼ cup (60ml) kecap manis
3 cups (480g) shredded cooked chicken

1 Place noodles in large heatproof bowl; cover with boiling water.
Separate noodles with fork; drain.
2 Heat oil in wok; stir-fry garlic, ginger and carrot until carrot is just tender.
Add prawns and curry powder; stir-fry until prawns change colour.
3 Add noodles and remaining ingredients; stir-fry until hot.

on the table in 25 minutes
serves 4 **per serving** 19.1g total fat (6.4g saturated fat); 2057kJ
(492 cal); 27.3g carbohydrate; 49.1g protein; 5.8g fibre

Chicken laksa

250g fresh egg noodles
1 teaspoon peanut oil
¼ cup (75g) laksa paste
3¼ cups (800ml) light coconut milk
1 litre (4 cups) chicken stock
2 tablespoons lime juice
1 tablespoon white sugar
1 tablespoon fish sauce
6 kaffir lime leaves, torn
2½ cups (425g) coarsely chopped cooked chicken
1 cup (80g) bean sprouts
½ cup loosely packed fresh vietnamese mint leaves

1 Rinse noodles in strainer under hot running water. Separate noodles with fork; drain.
2 Heat oil in large saucepan; cook paste, stirring, until fragrant. Stir in coconut milk, stock, juice, sugar, sauce and lime leaves; bring to a boil. Reduce heat, simmer, covered, 3 minutes. Add chicken; stir until laksa is heated through.
3 Divide noodles among serving bowls. Ladle laksa over noodles; top with sprouts and mint, and a wedge of lime, if desired.

on the table in 30 minutes
serves 4 **per serving** 22.9g total fat (11.4g saturated fat); 1973kJ (472 cal); 51.0g carbohydrate; 39.4g protein; 2.3g fibre
tip you can substitute your favourite kind of noodle for the egg noodles.

Chicken and mushroom frittata

1 tablespoon olive oil
3 green onions, chopped finely
200g button mushrooms, sliced thinly
1 medium tomato (150g), chopped finely
2½ cups (425g) coarsely chopped cooked chicken
2 tablespoons coarsely chopped fresh flat-leaf parsley
6 eggs, beaten lightly
2 cups (250g) coarsely grated cheddar cheese

1 Heat oil in large frying pan; cook onion and mushroom, stirring, until soft. Add tomato; cook until most of the liquid evaporates.
2 Stir in chicken and parsley. Pour egg over chicken mixture, sprinkle with cheese; cook over low heat until just set. Place pan under heated grill until cheese melts and frittata is browned lightly.
3 Cut frittata into wedges to serve.

on the table in 30 minutes
serves 6 **per serving** 16.8g total fat (5.5g saturated fat); 1333kJ (319 cal); 1.5g carbohydrate; 39.7g protein; 1.4g fibre

Thai chicken salad

350g yellow string beans, trimmed, halved
1 teaspoon finely grated lime rind
2 tablespoons lime juice
1 tablespoon grated palm sugar
1 clove garlic, crushed
1 tablespoon peanut oil
½ cup finely chopped fresh mint
2 teaspoons sweet chilli sauce
1 tablespoon fish sauce
3 cups (480g) shredded cooked chicken
250g cherry tomatoes, halved
1 cup coarsely chopped fresh coriander
1 fresh small red thai chilli, chopped finely

1 Boil, steam or microwave beans until almost tender. Rinse under cold water; drain.
2 Combine rind, juice, sugar, garlic, oil, mint and sauces in large bowl. Add beans, chicken, tomato and three-quarters of the coriander; toss gently to combine.
3 Top salad with remaining coriander and chilli just before serving.

on the table in 20 minutes
serves 4 **per serving** 14.1g total fat (3.6g saturated fat); 1246kJ (298 cal); 7.9g carbohydrate; 32.8g protein; 3.9g fibre
tip chopped snake beans can be substituted for the yellow string beans.

Chicken, zucchini and corn soup

20g butter
1 large brown onion (200g), chopped finely
1 clove garlic, crushed
2 medium zucchini (240g), grated coarsely
1 litre (4 cups) chicken stock
420g can creamed corn
2½ cups (425g) coarsely chopped cooked chicken
½ cup (125ml) cream

1 Melt butter in large saucepan; cook onion and garlic, stirring, until onion softens. Add zucchini; cook, stirring, 1 minute.
2 Add stock to pan; bring to a boil. Stir in corn and chicken; reduce heat, simmer, uncovered, until chicken is hot. Stir in cream just before serving.

on the table in 20 minutes
serves 4 **per serving** 27.6g total fat (14.5g saturated fat); 2023kJ (484 cal); 23.9g carbohydrate; 33.0g protein; 5.3g fibre

Chicken and lime noodle salad

250g bean thread noodles
1 medium carrot (120g)
1 lebanese cucumber (130g), halved, seeded
2 green onions, sliced thinly
1 medium red capsicum (200g), sliced thinly
3 cups (480g) shredded cooked chicken
½ cup loosely packed vietnamese mint leaves
½ cup loosely packed fresh coriander leaves
3 fresh small red thai chillies, sliced thinly
2 cloves garlic, crushed
⅓ cup (80ml) lime juice
⅓ cup (80ml) peanut oil
2 tablespoons fish sauce
1 tablespoon white sugar

1 Place noodles in large heatproof bowl; cover with boiling water.
Stand until tender; drain.
2 Using vegetable peeler, slice carrot and cucumber into ribbons.
3 Combine noodles, carrot and cucumber in large bowl with onion,
capsicum, chicken, mint, coriander, chilli and combined remaining
ingredients; toss gently to combine.

on the table in 15 minutes
serves 4 **per serving** 38.5g total fat (11.3g saturated fat); 2847kJ
(681 cal); 42.4g carbohydrate; 37.7g protein; 7.7g fibre
tips for an even more refreshing salad, refrigerate the drained noodles
overnight before combining with remaining ingredients. Substitute regular
mint or add extra coriander if you can't find vietnamese mint.

Baked pasta and chicken carbonara

250g spaghetti
1 tablespoon olive oil
500g button mushrooms, quartered
2 cloves garlic, crushed
1 teaspoon chopped fresh thyme
¼ cup (60ml) dry white wine
¾ cup (180ml) chicken stock
425g jar carbonara sauce
3 green onions, sliced thickly
3 cups (480g) shredded cooked chicken
⅔ cup (50g) finely grated parmesan cheese
⅓ cup (25g) stale breadcrumbs

1 Cook pasta in large saucepan of boiling water, uncovered, until just tender; drain. Rinse under cold running water; drain.
2 Preheat oven to 240°C/220°C fan-forced. Lightly oil 3-litre (12-cup) baking dish.
3 Meanwhile, heat oil in large frying pan; cook mushrooms, garlic and thyme, stirring, until mushrooms are lightly browned. Add wine and stock; bring to a boil. Cook, stirring, about 5 minutes or until liquid is reduced by half; remove from heat.
4 Add pasta to mushroom mixture with sauce, onion, chicken and half of the cheese; toss gently to combine.
5 Combine remaining cheese and breadcrumbs in small bowl. Pour pasta mixture into baking dish; sprinkle top with breadcrumb mixture. Bake, uncovered, about 10 minutes or until top is lightly browned.

on the table in 35 minutes
serves 4 **per serving** 28.8g total fat (8.6g saturated fat); 2926kJ (700 cal); 53.1g carbohydrate; 50.3g protein; 8.1g fibre

Crunchy chicken salad

3 cups (480g) shredded cooked chicken
1 small wombok (700g), sliced thinly
2 green onions, sliced thinly
100g mixed bean sprouts
½ cup firmly packed fresh coriander leaves
½ cup (75g) salted cashews
2 tablespoons toasted pepitas
soy dressing
¼ cup (60ml) soy sauce
⅓ cup (80ml) rice vinegar
2 tablespoons peanut oil
2 teaspoons brown sugar
1 teaspoon sesame oil

1 Make soy dressing.
2 Place chicken in large bowl with remaining salad ingredients. Drizzle dressing over salad; toss gently to combine.
soy dressing place ingredients in screw-top jar; shake well.

on the table in 15 minutes
serves 4 **per serving** 31.1g total fat (6.0g saturated fat); 1940kJ (464 cal); 7.5g carbohydrate; 36.4g protein; 5.1g fibre

Thai chicken in lettuce-leaf cups

8 large iceberg lettuce leaves
1 tablespoon kecap manis
1 teaspoon sesame oil
1 tablespoon lime juice
1 large zucchini (150g), grated coarsely
1 medium carrot (120g), grated coarsely
2 green onions, sliced thinly
1 medium red capsicum (200g), sliced thinly
3 cups (480g) shredded cooked chicken
1 tablespoon finely chopped fresh mint
2 tablespoons chopped fresh coriander
2 tablespoons sweet chilli sauce

1 Trim lettuce-leaf edges with scissors. Place leaves in large bowl of iced water; refrigerate.
2 Combine kecap manis, oil and juice in large bowl. Add zucchini, carrot, onion, capsicum, chicken, mint and half of the coriander; toss gently to combine.
3 Dry lettuce; divide leaves among serving plates. Top with chicken mixture; drizzle with combined sweet chilli sauce and remaining coriander.

on the table in 20 minutes
serves 4 **per serving** 10.7g total fat (2.8g saturated fat); 1095kJ (262 cal); 7.5g carbohydrate; 32.3g protein; 3.0g fibre

Chicken tostadas

4 large flour tortillas
½ cup (120g) canned refried beans
½ cup (130g) bottled medium chunky salsa
2½ cups (425g) coarsely chopped cooked chicken
1½ cups (185g) grated cheddar cheese
4 cups (240g) finely shredded iceberg lettuce
2 medium tomatoes (300g), chopped coarsely
3 green onions, sliced thinly
½ cup (120g) light sour cream

1 Preheat grill to hot.
2 Place tortillas, in single layer, on oven trays.
3 Combine beans and salsa in small bowl. Divide bean mixture among tortillas; top with chicken and cheese. Place under preheated grill until cheese melts and tortillas' edges crisp.
4 Top tostadas with lettuce, tomato, onion and sour cream to serve.

on the table in 25 minutes
serves 4 **per serving** 25.8g total fat (11.8g saturated fat); 2324kJ (556 cal); 33.9g carbohydrate; 44.2g protein; 5.4g fibre
tips refried beans are sold, canned, in most supermarkets, as are packaged flour tortillas. Made of pinto beans that are just parboiled then fried with various seasonings, refried beans are also known by their Mexican name of frijoles refritos. You will need to purchase one small iceberg lettuce for this recipe.

Chicken lavash rolls

1 cup (170g) coarsely chopped cooked chicken
1½ cups (90g) shredded iceberg lettuce
⅔ cup (200g) tzatziki dip
4 pieces lavash bread
greek salad
½ medium green cucumber (85g), chopped
1 medium tomato (150g), chopped
25g fetta cheese, chopped
2 tablespoons halved, seeded black olives
2 teaspoons lemon juice
2 teaspoons olive oil

1 Make greek salad.
2 Divide chicken, greek salad, lettuce and tzatziki among lavash;
roll up to enclose filling.
greek salad place ingredients in medium bowl; toss gently to combine.

on the table in 20 minutes
serves 2 **per serving** 28.0g total fat (8.9g saturated fat); 3164kJ
(757 cal); 77.7g carbohydrate; 43.6g protein; 8.7g fibre
tip tzatziki is a yogurt, cucumber and garlic dip available from most
supermarkets and delicatessens.

Chicken and asparagus pasta salad

500g macaroni
250g asparagus, trimmed, chopped coarsely
3 cups (480g) shredded cooked chicken
200g button mushrooms, sliced
⅓ cup chopped fresh chives
⅓ cup (85g) light sour cream
½ cup (150g) mayonnaise
1 tablespoon lemon juice
1 tablespoon wholegrain mustard

1 Cook pasta in large saucepan of boiling water, uncovered, until just tender; drain.
2 Meanwhile, boil, steam or microwave asparagus until just tender; drain.
3 Place pasta and asparagus in large bowl with chicken, mushrooms and chives.
4 Combine sour cream, mayonnaise, juice and mustard in small bowl or jug. Add to pasta mixture; toss gently to combine.

on the table in 25 minutes
serves 4 **per serving** 27.1g total fat (8.9g saturated fat); 2713kJ (649 cal); 55.4g carbohydrate; 43.2g protein; 4.8g fibre

Chicken chilli pizza

4 x 125g pizza bases
2 tablespoons tomato paste
1 tablespoon barbecue sauce
1½ teaspoons sambal oelek
1 clove garlic, crushed
1 cup (170g) coarsely chopped cooked chicken
100g button mushrooms, sliced thickly
1 small tomato (130g), halved, sliced thinly
1½ cups (165g) grated pizza cheese
2 teaspoons fresh thyme leaves

1 Preheat oven to 220°C/200°C fan-forced.
2 Place pizza bases on oven tray. Combine paste, sauce, sambal oelek and garlic in small bowl; spread evenly over bases.
3 Divide chicken, mushroom, tomato and cheese among bases.
4 Cook, uncovered, about 20 minutes or until pizza bases are crisp. Top with thyme.

on the table in 30 minutes
serves 4 **per serving** 16.4g total fat (6.8g saturated fat); 2445kJ (585 cal); 71.1g carbohydrate; 34.1g protein; 6.3g fibre
tips ready-made pizza bases are available in all supermarkets and fresh ones can be found at some bakeries. Pizza cheese is a convenient blend of coarsely grated processed cheddar, mozzarella and parmesan cheeses available from your supermarket.

Chicken with cacciatore-style sauce

1 tablespoon olive oil
1 medium brown onion (150g), chopped finely
2 cloves garlic, crushed
1 tablespoon tomato paste
2 x 400g cans tomatoes
½ cup (125ml) dry red wine
2 bay leaves
4 anchovy fillets, drained, chopped finely
1 cup (120g) seeded kalamata olives
2 tablespoons fresh oregano leaves
1 large barbecue chicken (900g), quartered, skinned

1 Heat oil in large saucepan; cook onion and garlic, stirring, until
onion softens. Add paste, undrained crushed tomatoes, wine,
bay leaves, anchovy and olives; bring to a boil. Reduce heat,
simmer, uncovered, 5 minutes.
2 Discard bay leaves; stir oregano through sauce. Add chicken;
stir until heated through. Serve sauce with penne pasta, if desired.

on the table in 30 minutes
serves 4 **per serving** 22.9g total fat (5.8g saturated fat); 2249kJ
(538 cal); 15.7g carbohydrate; 60.1g protein; 3.7g fibre

Chicken caesar salad

100g parmesan cheese
1 egg
1 clove garlic, quartered
2 tablespoons lemon juice
½ teaspoon dijon mustard
10 anchovy fillets, drained
¾ cup (180ml) olive oil
1 large cos lettuce, torn
2½ cups (425g) coarsely chopped cooked chicken
170g packet croutons

1 Using a vegetable peeler, slice cheese into thin ribbons.
2 Blend or process egg, garlic, juice, mustard and half of the anchovy until smooth. With motor operating, add oil in a thin, steady stream; process until dressing just thickens.
3 Place cheese in large bowl with lettuce, chicken, croutons and remaining anchovy; toss gently to combine.
4 Serve salad drizzled with dressing.

on the table in 25 minutes
serves 4 **per serving** 77.0g total fat (18.4g saturated fat); 4136kJ (987 cal); 19.3g carbohydrate; 54.5g protein; 5.7g fibre

Fried rice

2 teaspoons vegetable oil
2 eggs, beaten lightly
1 cup (125g) frozen peas
1 cup (160g) frozen corn kernels
2½ cups (425g) coarsely chopped cooked chicken
5 cups cooked long-grain white rice
6 green onions, chopped coarsely
¼ cup (60ml) soy sauce
2 tablespoons chopped fresh flat-leaf parsley
⅓ cup (80ml) sweet chilli sauce

1 Heat half of the oil in large heated wok. Pour egg into wok; cook over medium heat, tilting wok, until almost set. Remove omelette from wok; roll tightly, slice thinly.
2 Heat remaining oil in wok; stir-fry peas and corn until hot. Add chicken; stir-fry until hot. Add rice, onion, soy sauce and parsley; stir-fry until hot.
3 Serve fried rice topped with omelette and sweet chilli sauce.

on the table in 20 minutes
serves 6 **per serving** 9.7g total fat (2.4g saturated fat); 1760kJ (421 cal); 54.3g carbohydrate; 26.1g protein; 4.2g fibre
tip you will need to cook about 1⅔ cups (330g) rice for this recipe.

Moroccan chicken with couscous

1 cup (250ml) vegetable stock
1½ cups (300g) couscous
1 medium red onion (170g), sliced thinly
3 cups (480g) shredded cooked chicken
½ cup (75g) coarsely chopped dried apricots
½ cup (80g) sultanas
¼ cup finely chopped fresh mint
1 tablespoon pine nuts
2 teaspoons cumin seeds
¾ cup (180ml) bottled fat-free french dressing

1 Bring stock to a boil in large saucepan; remove from heat. Stir in couscous. Cover; stand about 5 minutes or until stock is absorbed, fluffing with fork.
2 Add onion, chicken, apricot, sultanas and mint to couscous; toss gently to combine.
3 Dry-fry pine nuts and seeds in small frying pan over low heat until just fragrant. Add to couscous with dressing; toss gently to combine.

on the table in 20 minutes
serves 4 **per serving** 22.7g total fat (4.2g saturated fat); 3093kJ (740 cal); 88.3g carbohydrate; 42.3g protein; 4.2g fibre

Greek chicken salad

375g small shell pasta
¼ cup coarsely chopped fresh oregano
½ cup (125ml) olive oil
¼ cup (60ml) lemon juice
3 cups (480g) shredded cooked chicken
1 medium red onion (170g), sliced thinly
500g cherry tomatoes, quartered
2 lebanese cucumbers (260g), chopped coarsely
1 cup (120g) seeded kalamata olives
1 large green capsicum (350g), chopped coarsely
280g jar marinated artichoke hearts, drained, chopped coarsely
200g fetta cheese, chopped coarsely

1 Cook pasta in large saucepan of boiling water, uncovered, until just tender; drain. Rinse under cold water; drain.
2 Meanwhile, place 2 tablespoons of the oregano with oil and juice in screw-top jar; shake well.
3 Place pasta in large bowl with chicken, onion, tomato, cucumber, olives, capsicum, artichoke, cheese and dressing; toss gently to combine.
4 Serve salad topped with remaining oregano.

on the table in 25 minutes
serves 4 **per serving** 37.7g total fat (12.8g saturated fat); 3754kJ (898 cal); 82.0g carbohydrate; 52.6g protein; 9.0g fibre
tips you can use your favourite kind of pasta for this recipe. Use the oil from the artichokes to make the dressing if you wish.

Barbecue-flavoured chicken and onions

2 tablespoons lemon juice
2 tablespoons brown sugar
1 tablespoon honey
1 clove garlic, crushed
¼ cup (60ml) soy sauce
2 medium brown onions (300g)
1 large barbecued chicken (900g), quartered

1 Preheat oven to 200°C/180°C fan-forced.
2 Combine juice, sugar, honey, garlic and sauce in small jug.
3 Chop onions into wedges. Place chicken and onion in shallow baking dish; pour over half the glaze mixture.
4 Bake, uncovered, about 20 minutes or until chicken is crisp and heated through, brushing frequently with remaining glaze mixture.

on the table in 30 minutes
serves 4 **per serving** 9.9g total fat (2.8g saturated fat); 1225kJ (293 cal); 16.7g carbohydrate; 33.5g protein; 1.1g fibre

Chicken, witlof and cashew salad

1 medium witlof (125g)
2 baby cos lettuces
1 medium yellow capsicum (200g), sliced thinly
1 small red onion (100g), sliced thinly
1 cup (150g) roasted unsalted cashews
3 cups (480g) shredded cooked chicken
dressing
1 cup (280g) yogurt
2 cloves garlic, crushed
2 teaspoons finely grated lemon rind
¼ cup (60ml) lemon juice
¼ cup coarsely chopped fresh coriander

1 Make dressing.
2 Trim and discard 1cm from base of witlof; separate leaves. Trim core from lettuce; separate leaves.
3 Place witlof and lettuce in large bowl with capsicum, onion, cashews and chicken. Pour dressing over salad; toss gently to combine.
dressing place ingredients in screw-top jar; shake well.

on the table in 20 minutes
serves 4 **per serving** 31.0g total fat (7.3g saturated fat); 2136kJ (511 cal); 14.7g carbohydrate; 42.0g protein; 5.8g fibre

Satay pizza with rocket and raita

½ cup (140g) crunchy peanut butter
½ cup (125ml) sweet chilli sauce
4 x 15cm pizza bases
3 cups (480g) shredded cooked chicken
200g provolone cheese, grated coarsely
50g baby rocket leaves
raita
1 lebanese cucumber (130g), chopped finely
1 small brown onion (80g), chopped finely
½ cup (140g) yogurt
2 tablespoons finely chopped fresh mint
1 long green chilli, chopped finely

1 Preheat oven to 200°C/180°C fan-forced.
2 Combine peanut butter and chilli sauce in small bowl.
3 Place pizza bases on oven trays; spread sauce mixture evenly over each base. Divide chicken and cheese among bases; cook about 15 minutes or until pizza tops brown and bases crisp.
4 Meanwhile, make raita.
5 Serve pizza topped with raita and rocket.
raita combine ingredients in small bowl.

on the table in 35 minutes
serves 4 **per serving** 48.1g total fat (16.3g saturated fat); 4301kJ (1029 cal); 73.1g carbohydrate; 70.5g protein; 10.6g fibre
tip ready-made pizza bases are available in all supermarkets and fresh ones can be found at some bakeries.

Fettuccine boscaiola with chicken

500g fettuccine pasta
1 tablespoon olive oil
1 medium brown onion (150g), chopped finely
2 rashers rindless bacon (125g), chopped finely
200g button mushrooms, sliced thinly
¼ cup (60ml) dry white wine
⅔ cup (160ml) cream
1 cup (250ml) milk
1 cup (170g) thinly sliced cooked chicken
¼ cup (20g) finely grated parmesan cheese
2 tablespoons coarsely chopped fresh flat-leaf parsley

1 Cook pasta in large saucepan of boiling water, uncovered, until just tender; drain, reserving ½ cup of cooking liquid.
2 Meanwhile, heat oil in large saucepan; cook onion, stirring, until soft. Add bacon and mushrooms; cook, stirring, 1 minute.
3 Add wine, cream and milk; bring to a boil. Reduce heat, simmer, stirring, 5 minutes. Add chicken; stir until combined.
4 Add pasta, cheese, parsley and reserved cooking liquid; toss gently over low heat until hot.

on the table in 20 minutes
serves 4 **per serving** 35.6g total fat (17.6g saturated fat); 3754kJ (898 cal); 94.6g carbohydrate; 42.9g protein; 8.1g fibre
tip fresh basil can be used instead of parsley, if you prefer.

Chicken, basil and wombok salad

3 cups (480g) shredded cooked chicken
4 cups (320g) finely shredded wombok
4 green onions, sliced thinly
¼ cup chopped fresh basil
1 clove garlic, crushed
¼ cup (60ml) peanut oil
¼ cup (60ml) lime juice
2 tablespoons fish sauce
1 tablespoon white sugar

1 Place chicken, wombok, onion and basil in large bowl.
2 Place garlic, oil, juice, sauce and sugar in screw-top jar; shake well.
3 Drizzle dressing over salad; toss gently to combine.

on the table in 15 minutes
serves 4 **per serving** 22.9g total fat (5.1g saturated fat); 1488kJ
(356 cal); 5.5g carbohydrate; 31.5g protein; 1.6g fibre
tip you will need to purchase a medium wombok for this recipe.

Chicken and sweet soy stir-fry

450g hokkien noodles
1 tablespoon peanut oil
3 cups (480g) coarsely chopped cooked chicken
6 green onions, sliced
1 clove garlic, crushed
2 cups (160g) bean sprouts
½ cup (125ml) chicken stock
2 tablespoons sweet chilli sauce
¼ cup (60ml) kecap manis

1 Place noodles in small heatproof bowl; cover with boiling water, separate with fork, drain.
2 Heat oil in wok; stir-fry chicken, onion and garlic until chicken is heated through.
3 Add noodles and sprouts to wok with combined stock, sauce and kecap manis; stir-fry until noodles are heated through.

on the table in 15 minutes
serves 4 **per serving** 14.8g total fat (3.7g saturated fat); 1789kJ (428 cal); 32.8g carbohydrate; 38.2g protein; 4.1g fibre

Chicken pasta salad

200g pasta shells
2½ cups (425g) chopped cooked chicken
250g cherry tomatoes, halved
1 small red capsicum (150g), chopped coarsely
6 green onions, sliced thickly
½ cup (80g) kalamata olives, seeded
400g can artichoke hearts, drained, halved
¼ cup shredded fresh basil
dressing
⅓ cup (80ml) lemon juice
1 tablespoon olive oil
1 tablespoon red wine vinegar
1 teaspoon white sugar
2 teaspoons wholegrain mustard

1 Cook pasta in large saucepan of boiling water, uncovered, until just
tender; drain. Rinse under cold running water; drain.
2 Meanwhile, make dressing.
3 Place pasta in large bowl with chicken and remaining salad ingredients.
Drizzle dressing over salad; toss gently to combine.
dressing place ingredients in screw-top jar; shake well.

on the table in 25 minutes
serves 4 **per serving** 15.2g total fat (3.5g saturated fat); 1960kJ
(469 cal); 45.7g carbohydrate; 34.4g protein; 4.6g fibre
tip use your favourite pasta shape for this salad, or use rice instead.

Tagliatelle, chicken and peas in mustard cream sauce

250g tagliatelle pasta
1 tablespoon olive oil
1 medium brown onion (150g), chopped finely
2 cloves garlic, crushed
½ cup (125ml) dry white wine
1 tablespoon dijon mustard
1 cup (250ml) cream
2 cups (250g) frozen peas, thawed
3 cups (480g) shredded cooked chicken
¼ cup finely chopped fresh garlic chives

1 Cook pasta in large saucepan of boiling water, uncovered, until just tender; drain.
2 Meanwhile, heat oil in large saucepan; cook onion and garlic, stirring, until onion softens. Add wine and mustard; bring to a boil. Reduce heat, simmer, uncovered, 5 minutes. Stir in cream; return mixture to a boil, then simmer again, uncovered, about 5 minutes or until sauce thickens slightly. Stir in drained peas and chicken; stir over low heat until mixture is hot.
3 Place pasta and chives in pan with chicken and pea sauce; toss gently to combine.

on the table in 30 minutes
serves 4 **per serving** 41.6g total fat (21.1g saturated fat); 3252kJ (778 cal); 50.7g carbohydrate; 42.2g protein; 6.7g fibre

glossary

allspice also known as pimento or jamaican pepper.

bacon rashers also known as bacon slices; made from cured and smoked pork side.

barbecue sauce spicy, tomato-based sauce used to marinate, baste or as an accompaniment.

basil, holy also known as kra pao or hot basil; different from thai and sweet basil, having an almost hot, spicy flavour similar to clove.

bean sprouts also known as bean shoots; tender new growths of assorted beans and seeds germinated for consumption as sprouts.

breadcrumbs

fresh bread, usually white, processed into crumbs.

packaged prepared fine-textured, crunchy white breadcrumbs.

stale crumbs made by grating or processing 1- or 2-day-old bread.

broad beans also called fava, windsor and horse beans; available dried, fresh, canned and frozen. Fresh should be peeled twice (discarding the outer long green pod and the beige-green tough inner shell); the frozen beans have had their pods removed but the beige shell still needs removal.

broccolini a cross between broccoli and chinese kale. Looks like broccoli but is milder and sweeter in taste.

buk choy also known as bok choy, pak choi, chinese white cabbage or chinese chard; has a fresh, mild mustard taste. Use both stems and leaves.

burghul also known as bulghur wheat; hulled steamed wheat kernels that, once dried, are crushed into various size grains. Burghul is not the same thing as cracked wheat (the untreated whole wheat berry broken during milling into a cereal product of varying degrees of coarseness).

butter we use salted butter unless stated otherwise; 125g is equal to 1 stick (4 ounces).

buttermilk low in fat, varying between 0.6 and 2.0 per cent per 100ml. The term originally given to the slightly sour liquid left after butter was churned from cream, today it is intentionally made from no-fat or low-fat milk to which specific bacterial cultures have been added during the manufacturing process. Available from the dairy section in supermarkets.

capers the grey-green buds of a warm climate (usually Mediterranean) shrub, sold either dried and salted or pickled in a vinegar brine.

capsicum also known as pepper or bell pepper.

cardamom a spice native to India and used extensively in its cuisine; can be purchased in pod, seed or ground form. Has a distinctive aromatic, sweetly rich flavour and is one of the world's most expensive spices.

cayenne pepper a thin-fleshed, long, extremely hot, dried red chilli, usually ground.

cheese

blue mould-treated cheese mottled with blue veining. Varieties include firm and crumbly stilton types and mild, creamy brie-like cheeses.

cheddar most common cow-milk tasty cheese; should be aged, hard and have a pronounced bite. We use a version having no more than 20 per cent fat when calling for low-fat cheese.

fetta a crumbly textured goat- or sheep-milk cheese having a sharp, salty taste. Ripened and stored in salted whey; particularly good cubed and tossed into salads. We use a version having no more than 15 per cent fat when calling for low-fat cheese.

fontina a smooth, firm Italian cow-milk cheese

with a creamy, nutty taste and brown or red rind; an ideal melting or grilling cheese.

gruyère a hard-rind Swiss cheese with small holes and a nutty, slightly salty flavour.

haloumi a Greek Cypriot cheese with a semi-firm, spongy texture and very salty yet sweet flavour. Ripened and stored in salted whey; it's best grilled or fried, and holds its shape well on being heated. Should be eaten while still warm as it becomes tough and rubbery on cooling.

mozzarella soft, spun-curd cheese; originating in southern Italy and traditionally made from water-buffalo milk, now it's generally made from cow milk. Is the most popular pizza cheese because of its low melting point and elasticity when heated. We use a version having no more than 17.5 per cent fat when calling for low-fat cheese.

parmesan also called parmigiano, parmesan is a hard, grainy cow-milk cheese originating in the Parma region of Italy. The curd is salted in brine for a month before being aged for up to 2 years, preferably in humid conditions.

pizza a commercial blend of grated cheddar, mozzarella and parmesan.

provolone a mild stretched-curd cheese similar to mozzarella when young, becoming hard, spicy and grainy the longer it's aged. Golden yellow in colour, with a smooth waxy rind, provolone is a good all-purpose cheese.

ricotta a soft, sweet, moist, white cow-milk cheese with a low fat content (about 8.5 per cent) and slightly grainy texture. It roughly translates as "cooked again" and refers to ricotta's manufacture from a whey that is itself a by-product of other cheese making.

chicken

barbecued sold already cooked; available from supermarkets, delicatessens and chicken-speciality stores.

breast fillet all skin and bones removed. When a recipe calls for breast fillet, this is a single breast fillet.

drumettes the wing is trimmed to resemble a drumstick; tip of the bone chopped off.

drumstick leg with skin and bone intact.

lovely legs trimmed, skinned drumsticks.

maryland leg and thigh still connected in a single piece; bones and skin intact.

mince ground thigh or breast meat.

smoked ready-to-eat, available as whole small bird or breasts sold cryovac-packed in supermarkets.

tenderloin thin strip of meat lying just under the breast.

thigh cutlet thigh with skin and centre bone intact; sometimes found skinned with bone intact.

thigh fillets thigh with skin and bones removed.

wings the whole wing, bone and skin intact.

chickpeas also called garbanzos, hummus or channa; an irregularly round, sandy-coloured legume. Available canned or dried (dried chickpeas must be soaked in cold water for several hours before use).

chilli always use rubber gloves when handling fresh chillies as they can burn your skin. We use unseeded chillies as the seeds contain the heat.

jalapeño pronounced hah-lah-pain-yo. Fairly hot, medium-sized, plump, dark green chilli; available pickled, sold canned or bottled, and fresh.

sweet chilli sauce comparatively mild, fairly sticky and runny bottled sauce made from red chillies, sugar, garlic and white vinegar.

thai also called "scuds"; tiny, very hot and bright red in colour.

choy sum also called pakaukeo or flowering cabbage, a member of the buk choy family; has long stems, light green leaves and yellow flowers. Stems and leaves are both edible.

coconut cream obtained commercially from the first pressing of the coconut flesh alone, without the addition of water. Available in cans and cartons at most supermarkets.

coriander also called cilantro, pak chee or chinese parsley.

cornflour also known as cornstarch. Available made from corn or wheat.

couscous a fine, grain-like cereal product made from semolina; a semolina flour and water dough is sieved then dehydrated to produce minuscule even-sized pellets of couscous; it is rehydrated by steaming or by adding warm liquid. Swells to three or four times its original size.

cumin the dried seed of a plant related to the parsley family. Available dried as seeds or ground.

curly endive also called frisée; a prickly-looking, curly-leafed green vegetable having an edible white heart. Fairly bitter in flavour.

egg we use large eggs with an average weight of 60g unless stated otherwise. Some recipes call for raw or barely cooked eggs; exercise caution if there is a salmonella problem in your area, particularly in food eaten by children and pregnant women.

eggplant also known as aubergine.

fennel bulbs also called finocchio or anise; a crunchy green vegetable slightly resembling celery.

fish sauce called naam pla if Thai-made, nuoc naam if Vietnamese; the two are almost identical. Made from pulverised salted fermented fish (most often anchovies); has a pungent smell and strong taste. Use according to your taste.

five-spice powder ingredients vary from country to country; usually a blend of ground cinnamon, cloves, star anise, sichuan pepper and fennel seeds. Available from most supermarkets or Asian food shops.

gai lan also known as gai larn, chinese broccoli and chinese kale; green vegetable used more for its stems than its leaves.

galangal a root, similar to ginger in its use. It has a hot-sour ginger-citrusy flavour; used in fish curries and soups.

garam masala literally meaning blended spices; based on varying proportions of cloves, cardamom, cinnamon, coriander, fennel and cumin, roasted and ground together. Black pepper and chilli can be added for a hotter version.

ginger
fresh also called green or root ginger; the thick gnarled root of a tropical plant. Store, peeled, in a jar of dry sherry; refrigerate or freeze in an airtight container.

pickled pink or red in colour; available, packaged, from Asian food shops. Paper-thin shavings of ginger in a mixture of vinegar, sugar and natural colouring.

harissa a North African paste made from dried red chillies, garlic, olive oil and caraway seeds; can be used as a rub for meat, an ingredient in sauces and dressings, or as a condiment. Available ready-made from Middle Eastern food shops and some supermarkets.

hoisin a thick, sweet and spicy Chinese barbecue sauce made from salted fermented soybeans, onions and garlic; used as a baste or marinade.

kaffir lime leaves also called bai magrood, looks like two glossy dark green leaves joined end to end in a rounded hourglass shape. Fresh or dried, they're used like bay or curry leaves in many South-East Asian cuisines, especially Thai. Sold fresh, dried or frozen, dried leaves are less potent so double the number if using them as a substitute for fresh; a strip of fresh lime peel may be substituted for each kaffir lime leaf.

kecap manis a dark, thick sweet soy sauce used in most South-East Asian cuisines; its sweetness is derived from the addition of either molasses or palm sugar when brewed.

kumara the polynesian name of an orange-fleshed sweet potato.

lebanese cucumber short, slender and thin-skinned. Probably the most popular variety for its tender, edible skin, tiny, yielding seeds, and sweet, fresh taste.

lemon grass also called takrai, serai or serah. A tall, clumping, lemon-smelling and tasting, sharp-edged aromatic tropical grass; the white lower part of the stem is used, finely chopped.

marsala a fortified Italian wine identified by its intense amber colour and complex aroma.

mayonnaise we use whole-egg mayonnaise.

mesclun pronounced mess-kluhn. A blend of assorted young lettuce and other green leaves.

mirin a Japanese champagne-coloured cooking wine, made of glutinous rice and alcohol. It is used expressly for cooking and should not be confused with sake.

mizuna Japanese in origin; the frizzy green salad leaves have a delicate mustard flavour.

mushrooms
button small, cultivated white mushrooms with a mild flavour.
flat large, flat mushrooms with a rich earthy flavour, ideal for filling and barbecuing. They are sometimes misnamed field mushrooms which are wild mushrooms.
oyster also known as abalone; grey-white mushrooms shaped like a fan. Prized for their smooth texture and subtle, oyster-like flavour.
shiitake, fresh also called chinese black, forest or golden oak mushrooms. Although cultivated, they have the earthiness and taste of wild mushrooms.
swiss brown also called roman or cremini; light to dark brown mushrooms with full-bodied flavour.

mustard
black seeds also called brown mustard seeds; more pungent than the white variety; used frequently in curries.

dijon also called french. Pale brown, creamy, distinctively flavoured and fairly mild.
wholegrain made from crushed seeds and dijon-style french mustard.

noodles
bean thread also called cellophane, wun sen or glass noodles because they become transparent when cooked. White in colour, very delicate and fine. Must be soaked to soften before use; using them deep-fried requires no pre-soaking.
crisp fried egg noodles that have been deep-fried then packaged for sale on supermarket shelves.
dried rice stick also called dried rice noodles. Made from rice flour and water, available flat and wide or very thin (vermicelli). Must be soaked in boiling water to soften.
egg also called ba mee or yellow noodles; made from wheat flour and eggs, sold fresh or dried. Range in size from very fine strands to wide, spaghetti-like pieces as thick as a shoelace.
fresh rice come in strands of various widths or large sheets weighing about 500g, to be cut into the desired noodle size. Chewy and pure white, they do not need pre-cooking before use.

hokkien also called stir-fry noodles; fresh wheat noodles resembling thick, yellow-brown spaghetti needing no pre-cooking before use.

instant also known as 2-minute noodles; quick cooking noodles with flavour sachet.

rice vermicelli also called sen mee, mei fun or bee hoon. Similar to bean thread noodles, only longer and made with rice flour instead of mung bean starch. Before using, soak dried noodles in hot water until softened; boil briefly then rinse with hot water.

singapore pre-cooked wheat noodles best described as a thinner version of hokkien; sold, packaged, in the refrigerated section of supermarkets.

soba thin, pale-brown Japanese noodle; made from buckwheat and varying proportions of wheat flour. Available dried and fresh, and in flavoured varieties; eaten in soups, stir-fries and, chilled, on their own.

oil

olive made from ripened olives. Extra virgin and virgin are the first and second press, respectively, and are considered the best; the term 'extra light' or 'light' on other types refers to taste not fat levels.

peanut pressed from ground peanuts; the most commonly used oil in Asian cooking because of its capacity to handle high heat without burning.

sesame made from roasted, crushed, white sesame seeds; a flavouring rather than a cooking medium.

vegetable oils sourced from plant rather than animal fats.

onion

green also known as scallion or (incorrectly) shallot; an immature onion picked before the bulb has formed, having a long, bright-green edible stalk.

red also called spanish, red spanish or bermuda onion; a sweet-flavoured, large, purple-red onion.

shallots also called french shallots, golden shallots or eschalots. Small, elongated, brown-skinned members of the onion family; grow in tight clusters like garlic.

oyster sauce thick, richly flavoured brown sauce made from oysters and their brine; cooked with salt and soy sauce, and thickened with starches.

paprika ground dried sweet red capsicum.

pepitas dried pumpkin seeds; plain or salted.

pine nuts also known as pignoli.

plum sauce a thick, sweet and sour dipping sauce made from plums, vinegar, sugar, chillies and spices.

prawns also known as shrimp.

prosciutto an unsmoked Italian ham; salted, air-cured and aged, it is usually eaten uncooked.

radicchio Italian in origin; a member of the chicory family. Its dark burgundy leaves have a strong, bitter flavour. Can be cooked or eaten raw in salads.

rice paper also called banh trang. Made from rice flour and water then stamped into rounds; is quite brittle. Dip briefly in water, so they become pliable wrappers for food.

rocket also called arugula, rugula and rucola; peppery green leaf eaten raw in salads.

sambal oelek also ulek or olek; salty paste made from ground chillies and vinegar.

snow peas also called mangetout.

soy sauce made from fermented soybeans. We use Japanese soy sauce unless stated otherwise.

light thin in consistency; paler than others but the saltiest tasting; used when the ingredients' natural colour is to be maintained. Not to be confused with salt-reduced or low-sodium soy sauces.

spinach also known as english spinach and incorrectly, silverbeet.

star anise a dried star-shaped pod; seeds have an astringent aniseed flavour. Used to flavour stocks and marinades.

sugar
caster also known as superfine or finely granulated table sugar.
palm also called nam tan pip, jaggery, jawa or gula melaka; made from the sap of the sugar palm tree. Light brown to black in colour; usually sold in rock-hard cakes. If unavailable, use brown sugar.
white we use coarse, granulated table sugar unless stated otherwise.

sumac a purple-red, astringent ground spice; adds a tart, lemony flavour to dips and dressings and goes well with barbecued meat. Available from Middle Eastern food stores.

tamarind the tamarind tree produces clusters of hairy brown pods, each filled with seeds and a viscous pulp, that are dried and pressed into blocks. Gives a sweet-sour, slightly astringent taste to marinades, pastes, sauces and dressings. Available in Asian food shops. Tamarind paste (tamarind juice distilled into a condensed paste) is also available.

teriyaki sauce Japanese sauce made from soy sauce, mirin, sugar, ginger and spices.

tomato
canned whole peeled tomatoes in natural juices; available crushed, chopped or diced, and sometimes unsalted or reduced salt. Use in recipes undrained.
cherry also called tiny tim or tom thumb tomatoes; small and round.
egg also called plum or roma; smallish, oval-shaped tomatoes.
grape small, long oval-shaped tomatoes.
paste triple-concentrated tomato puree used to flavour soups, stews, sauces and casseroles.
puree canned pureed tomatoes (not paste); substitute with fresh peeled and pureed tomatoes.

tortilla thin, round unleavened bread originating in Mexico; avaiable frozen, fresh or vacuum-packed, made from wheat flour or corn.

turmeric is a rhizome related to galangal and ginger. Must be grated or pounded to release its aroma and pungent flavour. Known for the golden colour it imparts, fresh turmeric can be substituted with the more common dried powder.

vietnamese mint not a mint at all, but a pungent and peppery narrow-leafed member of the buckwheat family.

wasabi paste an Asian horseradish used to make the pungent, green-coloured sauce traditionally served with Japanese raw fish dishes.

water chestnuts resemble true chestnuts in appearance, hence the English name. Small brown tubers with a crisp, white, nutty-tasting flesh. Although best fresh, they're more easily obtained canned.

watercress belongs to the cress family, a large group of peppery greens used raw in salads, dips and sandwiches, or cooked in soups. Highly perishable, use as soon as possible.

witlof also known as belgian endive.

wombok also known as chinese cabbage, peking or napa cabbage; elongated in shape with pale green, crinkly leaves and is the most common cabbage in South-East Asia.

worcestershire sauce thin, dark-brown spicy sauce used as a seasoning for meat, gravies and cocktails, and as a condiment.

zucchini also known as courgette.

index

MEASURES

One Australian metric measuring cup holds approximately 250ml, one Australian metric tablespoon holds 20ml, one Australian metric teaspoon holds 5ml.

The difference between one country's measuring cups and another's is within a two- or three-teaspoon variance, and will not affect your cooking results.North America, New Zealand and the United Kingdom use a 15ml tablespoon.

All cup and spoon measurements are level. The most accurate way of measuring dry ingredients is to weigh them. When measuring liquids, use a clear glass or plastic jug with the metric markings.

We use large eggs with an average weight of 60g.

LIQUID MEASURES

METRIC	IMPERIAL
30ml	1 fluid oz
60ml	2 fluid oz
100ml	3 fluid oz
125ml	4 fluid oz
150ml	5 fluid oz (¼ pint/1 gill)
190ml	6 fluid oz
250ml	8 fluid oz
300ml	10 fluid oz (½ pint)
500ml	16 fluid oz
600ml	20 fluid oz (1 pint)
1000ml (1 litre)	1¾ pints

LENGTH MEASURES

METRIC	IMPERIAL
3mm	⅛in
6mm	¼in
1cm	½in
2cm	¾in
2.5cm	1in
5cm	2in
6cm	2½in
8cm	3in
10cm	4in
13cm	5in
15cm	6in
18cm	7in
20cm	8in
23cm	9in
25cm	10in
28cm	11in
30cm	12in (1ft)

DRY MEASURES

METRIC	IMPERIAL
15g	½oz
30g	1oz
60g	2oz
90g	3oz
125g	4oz (¼lb)
155g	5oz
185g	6oz
220g	7oz
250g	8oz (½lb)
280g	9oz
315g	10oz
345g	11oz
375g	12oz (¾lb)
410g	13oz
440g	14oz
470g	15oz
500g	16oz (1lb)
750g	24oz (1½lb)
1kg	32oz (2lb)

OVEN TEMPERATURES

These oven temperatures are only a guide for conventional ovens.
For fan-forced ovens, check the manufacturer's manual.

	°C (CELSIUS)	°F (FAHRENHEIT)	GAS MARK
Very slow	120	250	½
Slow	150	275 – 300	1 – 2
Moderately slow	160	325	3
Moderate	180	350 – 375	4 – 5
Moderately hot	200	400	6
Hot	220	425 – 450	7 – 8
Very hot	240	475	9

Editorial director Susan Tomnay
Creative director Hieu Chi Nguyen
Food director Pamela Clark
Food editor Louise Patniotis
Senior editor Stephanie Kistner
Designer Caryl Wiggins
Nutrition information Rebecca Squadrito
Director of sales Brian Cearnes
Marketing manager Bridget Cody
Production manager Cedric Taylor

Chief executive officer Ian Law
Group publisher Pat Ingram
General manager Christine Whiston
Editorial director (WW) Deborah Thomas

WW food team Lyndey Milan, Alexandra Elliott, Frances Abdallaoui

Produced by ACP Books, Sydney.
Printing by Toppan Printing Co., China
Published by ACP Books, a division of ACP Magazines Ltd,
54 Park St, Sydney; GPO Box 4088, Sydney, NSW 2001
phone +61 2 9282 8618 fax +61 2 9267 9438
acpbooks@acpmagazines.com.au www.acpbooks.com.au
To order books phone 136 116 (within Australia)
Send recipe enquiries to recipeenquiries@acpmagazines.com.au

RIGHTS ENQUIRIES
Laura Bamford, Director ACP Books
lbamford@acpuk.com

Australia Distributed by Network Services,
phone +61 2 9282 8777 fax +61 2 9264 3278
networkweb@networkservicescompany.com.au
United Kingdom Distributed by Australian Consolidated Press (UK),
phone (01604) 642 200 fax (01604) 642 300
books@acpuk.com
Canada Distributed by Whitecap Books Ltd,
phone (604) 980 9852 fax (604) 980 8197
customerservice@whitecap.ca www.whitecap.ca
New Zealand Distributed by Netlink Distribution Company, phone (9) 366 9966
ask@ndc.co.nz
South Africa Distributed by PSD Promotions,
phone (27 11) 392 6065/6/7 fax (27 11) 392 6079/80
orders@psdprom.co.za

Clark, Pamela.
The Australian Women's Weekly
Fast chicken
ISBN 978-1-86396-601-6
1. Cookery (Chicken).
I. Title. II. Title: Australian women's weekly.
© ACP Magazines Ltd 2007
ABN 18 053 273 546

Cover Sumac and paprika-spiced chicken with herb salad, page 97
Photographer Prue Ruscoe
Stylist Julz Beresford
Additional photography Chris Chen
Additional styling Stephanie Souvlis
Food preparation Nicole Jennings